RELEASE RESISTANCE

Liz Landon
Release Resistance

All rights reserved
Copyright © 2023 by Liz Landon

Published by BooxAi

ISBN: 978-965-578-094-9

RELEASE RESISTANCE

Allow Manifestations Through Powerful Perspective Shifts

Liz Landon

"Imagination is more important than knowledge. For knowledge is limited to all we now know and understand, while imagination embraces the entire world, and all there ever will be to know and understand."

— Albert Einstein

Contents

To my family who co-create my beautiful reality with me

To my inner being and her infinite intelligence and unconditional love

And to Hannah, my magnificent alignment partner

And to everyone living in the new paradigm

Most of all, to you, the reader, for being open and ready to the life you desire

"When people ask us how long does it take for something to manifest, we say, it takes as long as it takes you to release the RESISTANCE. Could be 30 years, could be 40 years, could be 50 years, could be a week. Could be tomorrow afternoon."

— Abraham Hicks

Foreword

How are you? Answering this very question truthfully to myself and to selective others is the crux of my entire existence. I have never told more lies than how I have responded to this three-worded question. I say I am fine, but really, all too often, I am not. I am divorced, middle-aged, struggling with an eating disorder, low self-worth, yet I tell most people I am fine. Most of us do. We lie and we all have our reasons. For me, this is my conditioned response so I protect others from my perceived burdens. I am also even guilty of saying I am fine with the intention that possibly someone would see it as a cry for help.

Because I am often blatantly dishonest concerning my well-being, I have spent the last three years going inward to explore and discover what I can do in my here and now to be ok. My journey is not about the response to others but about truly feeling better. I desire to know my true self and to reveal her as well. My outer consciousness, my brain, can often feel like a stroll in a bad neighborhood, it is very fear-based. My inner consciousness is a beautiful stroll in my goddess garden. My brain will sometimes tell me I am bad, people are bad, and possibly circumstances are bad. My inner being offers me peace from a place of absolute unconditional love. Within my anxious mind, there is crazy making, and within my inner soul, there is peace making. The discussions within my logical brain are ironically often unkind and illogical, the downloads from my inner being however are kind and logical. Needless to say, going on an inner journey to soothe my outer journey of suffering is how I find compassion for myself.

With this, I welcome you to my calibration portal. I come with the acceptance of being a master of the Universe where I know by going inward I tap into my own internal resources. By this, I choose to connect with my inner being daily by self-soothing my questions and wobbles from the essence of my desire to be steady. Meditation is personal, and for some it may be about reaching a point of nothingness, or simply allowing for stillness. I believe for all of us, meditative moments offer the space needed to move through our negative emotions. For myself specifically, it means to feel better through my imagination, visual imagery, and memory recall. The answers, which I refer to as divine downloads, allow for my own personal expansion. Every divine download is backed by infinite intelligence and unconditional love. Mind you, I so appreciate getting advice from my outer world but I am predominantly empowered from within. My internal being is a safe place created from my own acceptance that I have the power to practice thinking what I do want versus what I don't want. From a place where I am following only my inspired impulses, my nudge from the Universe is one where I show up as an uplifter. I am here to guide others towards personal growth and expansion by opening a safe space to dig deep into our wounds and allow for true healing as opposed to simple surface level healing. This is where my path feels lit up, this is my highest desire being shown to the world. How do I know this? Writing this book is one big HELL YES for me. Trust. Allow. Surrender to the beautiful forces of the Universe.

When it came to my own intellectuality, I was always encouraged to explore further, but when it came to my emotional state, I was taught to literally buck up buttercup, or to simply get on with it. I am here to say, it is vital for all of us to deal with our inner shit. If shit can happen in our physical worlds, then shifts can happen in our internal world. This is where mindgasms come in, when you allow for cognitive climaxes through reframing your thoughts, the release puts you in the vibrational vicinity of your desires. Our inner consciousness is where all of us have source energy…it is where you are offered clarity, empowerment, and vitality. I cordially invite my readers to embrace my teachings as a human resource guiding you towards the connection between you and source energy.

I recently heard Abraham Hicks, a channeled collective coalescence through Esther Hicks, say, "Imagination is the receiving mode," and when you are getting visual representations in our mind, you are experiencing the highest frequency. Through my experiences where I once talked about my life as a child of trauma to my new story of appreciating my juicy journey, I have internalized that how I am feeling is an indicator of what is coming up next in my life. I no longer try to make sense of my life, I simply live very aware of what my emotional and physical sensations are telling. From no longer making sense to feeling sensations creates a very intimate relationship with my whole being.

I know the Law of Attraction is going to respond to my emotions, whether they are negative or positive. That being the case, I now know that the desired life is not about toxic positivity but about feeling even a little bit better. By allowing better feeling emotions in, our minds can stop negative momentum and the Universe will respond to our highest desires as opposed to our lowest emotional responses.

From all of this birthed one of my most impactful affirmations of the last three years: If I have time to feel like shit, I have time to feel good.

This path has become one that feels like play, as I love to speak metaphorically. I find great pleasure in using imagery to express the intensity of my life's circumstances. When it comes to dealing with our inner shit, I think about my family packing up from a home we lived in for 20 years. I literally opened the junk drawer and turned it over right into the garbage. I did not sift or sort, I simply dumped the entire drawer out and proclaimed that our next house will not have one. Needless to say, our current home has one. That being said, our junk drawers can be completely cleaned out, we can even say we never have one, yet one eventually exists, and slowly it gets filled back up, even may get jammed, until we deal with it by cleaning it out. I share the analogy of the junk drawer to one's own mental drawer, we are all responsible for the maintenance of it. Ideally, you clean it out before it gets packed with things that no longer serve you. YES, our junk can be someone else's treasure, but in terms of our own mental junk, you have the ability to turn it all into an expansion for your own higher good. From the junk drawer to the treasure trove, this is where you discover your value, but it is entirely up to you. We have to take ownership and responsibility for our own growth because we can. My core belief is that all of us can shift or clear energies through visual imagery, all you have to have is the desire to feel better.

Carl Jung, Swiss psychologist and psychiatrist who founded analytic psychology, wrote, *"The creative aspect of the imagination frees us from our knowledge of the nothing but, and raises us to the state of one who plays."* **One who plays**, this also speaks to me because I believe life is meant to be a playground where we primarily experience joy. Jung's concept of active imagination has been described as a dreamlike state outside of the state of sleep, and for me, this occurs during meditation. When we quiet our mind and allow for nothingness, our outer consciousness is in the receiving mode for messages and guidance from our unconscious mind.

From my personal experience, the imagery can allow for interpretation that manifests itself as answers that soothe my state of being. My highest desire is to simply feel better knowing all outcomes are vibrational. Alignment, my vibration and my inner guidance system are my spiritual trifecta allowing the thoughts, feelings and emotions of my unconscious mind to have a healing effect on my outer being. This, in turn, alters my physical reality as I am able to follow my flow with ease, allowing my highest desires to feel effortless.

Ultimately, life has come full circle for me. As a child, I would escape my reality with picture books, daydreaming, and my imagination, and now I implement similar methods as an adult with the power of my mind.

This is my reminder to you that when we are living in duality, when we are living in polarity, and when we are living with split energy, we give out mixed signals to the Universe. In return, the Universe responds with mixed experiences that offer mixed emotions. We create with the power of our mind. Meditation is the fifth dimension that allows for a transcended state of consciousness, giving us further access to steadiness with our energies and the Universe.

From Trauma to Nirvana

What humans call imagination is what we already call doneness. You want to call it imagination - what it is is your realization of something that's coming. Your imagination is deciphering thoughts that haven't manifested yet.

— Abraham Hicks

I am a big fan of Abraham Hicks, who describe themselves as a group consciousness from the non-physical dimensions. They offer leading-edge teachings about the Law of Attraction. One excerpt I came across was about the idea that *The Law of Attraction Treats My Imagination as Reality:* The Universe, which is responding to the thoughts you are thinking, does not distinguish between a thought from your observation of some observed reality and a thought brought about by your imagination. In either case, the thought equals your point of attraction, and if you focus upon it long enough, it will become your reality. (Abraham-Hicks Law of Attraction Cards)

This excerpt spoke to me because I have used imagery to heal myself since I was a little girl. As I furthered myself into the studies of Abraham Hicks, even as a child, by harnessing the power of my mind and creating and recreating images in my mind, I have positively impacted my point of attraction. Embrace the idea of imagination from a place of alignment, often offered during meditation. From a state of alignment comes affirmations and thoughts flowing with momentum towards you, becoming a vibrational match to your desires.

As a child of poverty and trauma, where we did not have the funds for therapy, nor was I brave enough to ask for help, I became very accustomed to imagining my blues away. I loved picturing exactly what I desired to have happen in my life, I loved altering frightening images into safer ones, and I especially loved the escapism I would experience while daydreaming. From a very young age, I appreciated knowing that a beautiful reality existed within my subconscious, and with the vividness of my mind, I could play and feel better on a whim. This is my healing gift.

Now a retired educator and mom of two, I have had the pleasure of watching children of all ages play. The power of the imagination is active within all of us from a very young age. I have often found it to be unfortunate that daydreaming is seen as an unnecessary distraction, because I have a core belief that imagination is crucial to the development of cognitive abilities, problem solving skills and socialconsciousness. Fast forward to adulthood, my imagination has been my best coping mechanism during board meetings, road trips, and the most uncomfortable situations. I am able to stop negative emotional momentum by imagining and creating imagery towards my dreams and aspirations. If I can even allow for momentary feelings of satisfaction, relief and freedom, I know I am powerfully creating a better reality.

The imaginative exercises behind my meditative state can immediately induce a relaxation response where not only am I guided to imagery that soothes my soul, but I am also offered verbal guidance from within. Some may call this channeling, but I really believe it is being fully present, so you are tuned in to the verbal and visual vividness that the state of nothingness provides. At the beginning of the pandemic, I began to hone in on my imaginative powers more so than ever. During a very uncertain time, my whole being desired balance, and I have known since I was a child that guided imagery from within would offer the mind-body connection I craved. Through my own recent healing, I have embraced the centrality of imagery and tapping into personal memories through the life of my internal spirit. By quieting my mind through meditation and conversations from within, I can bridge between my human psyche and my infinite intelligence that exists within me at all times. This is my invitation to you to start favoring the path of least resistance by indulging in self-care throughout this guided imagery journey with me. When I say self-care, I am not talking about what we can do outwardly, but more importantly, how we care for ourselves inwardly. There are many of us that may have lacked nurturing adult attention while growing up, where self-isolation became our dominant coping skill. As so many of us have been left alone to deal with our emotions, we may or may not be stuck in a trauma cycle. What I now know to be true is by using the power of my mind, when I release what is no longer for me, I then receive what is. No more rinse and repeat with the negative emotions that were stuck on a repetitive loop of holding me hostage emotionally, through my imagination, I shifted towards release and receive. Allow your visual connectedness to be your conduit, your channel for conveying, releasing and receiving, both infinite intelligence and unconditional love.

Imagination + Vividness = Reality

There is no coming to consciousness without pain. People will do anything, no matter how absurd, in order to avoid facing their own soul. One does not become enlightened by imagining figures of light, but by making the darkness conscious.

— Carl Jung

In my early twenties as a counselor for at-risk youth, I had a printed out sign on my office door that read: Imagination + Vividness = Reality. The power of the mind has always been an obsession of mine. Where some people might say, SEEING IS BELIEVING, for me, it has always been BELIEVING IS SEEING. I believed my imagination would allow me to see and feel the life I desired, as a result I have always felt I can bend time and space reality. When I can feel better and see, hear, touch, smell and taste my desired reality in my here and now, I know I can bring in all that I manifest more quickly.

When I attended my Masters in Education program, we read Robert Fulghum's book "All I Need to Know I Learned in Kindergarten". The book reads: "I believe that imagination is stronger than knowledge. That myth is more potent than history. That dreams are more powerful than facts. That hope always triumphs over experience. That laughter is the only cure for grief. And I believe that love is stronger than death." When I read this, I knew I would go on to be an educator that allowed her students to daydream, and I did. I believe that our children need a fleeting form of escapism because when you are faced with the undesirable it is an opportunity to create a better life using your mind. I believe this to be true for adults as well.

As a teacher, I also loved exposing my students to the HAROLD and the PURPLE CRAYON book series. The premise of Harold and the Purple Crayon lends itself to a beautiful and philosophical discussion around the real in reality. In Harold's world, his surroundings are represented by a blank page and he is given carte blanche to create with his purple crayon. Whether Harold is creating from a place of make-believe or creating his desired reality, he is coming from a place of freedom to do so. When Harold desires to take a walk in the moonlight, he draws a moon. When there is no path to walk on, he draws one. Harold interacts with his drawings in a very real way, and I can say that I also interact with my imagination in a very real way. Whereas Harold holds a big purple crayon to create with, we hold the power of our mind. We are all powerful creators.

I believe the vastness of human awareness lies under the surface of everyday consciousness and that we suppress it. In darkness, there is light, and this journey can be very revealing, healing and liberating. Suffice to say, see your personal IMAGINE NATION to be a nation of sacred space, where you imagine-ate, imagine and create the life you desire. Through meditation and imagination, you can accept yourself and open up more capacity for growth and expansion.

There are people in my life who have asked me how I use my imagination to visualize. My response is shocking because I begin by bringing my perceived trauma or my life's hot topic to the forefront of my mind. I allow all of the negative emotions in until I am fully activated, then I begin to quiet my mind by bringing in imagery that feels better. My healing is enhanced by imagining being inside of myself and looking out through the eyes of God, Source, my inner being at the ideal result. My visual journeys guide me to feeling better. When I speak of Source energy, I am speaking of a very chilled out state of being. As Abraham Hicks beautifully states, 'Source knows the path is inevitable and unfolding, and you're intuitive and you're right on it. All is well and things are always working out for you. Source knows the perfection of where you stand. You have to keep talking yourself into alignment. That's the work. That's the allowing.'

Living in alignment is not about our lives being effort *none*, but effortless, a life that feels like less work because you are tuned in and following your inspired impulses. I believe imagery healing through meditation offers our intuitive thoughts to be more accessible. We then are always moving in the right direction because when you feel good, your inner guidance system is allowing the Universe to respond to your higher vibration.

With this, I bring so much appreciation to the divine energies within me. Imagination + Vividness= Reality is a transformational formula. As we grow up, we unfortunately tend to use our imagination less, but this book asks us to challenge that and bring our imaginative states back as a state of healing. Your vibrational habits and patterns go where you go, and personally, I love knowing I can feel better in my here and now. Positive aspects found in visual imagery will activate more positive aspects in your human experience. Simply put, we are being solution-oriented and not problem-focused and this will help close the gap from where you are towards where you want to be.

The greatest discovery of my generation is that human beings, by changing their inner attitudes of their minds, can change the outer aspects of their lives.

— William James

Ineffable

I feel very inspired to share the word, ineffable. I spent my first fifty years never having heard of this word, a word used to express and peak one's personal expansion. Ineffable, nirvana, expansion, and even peace were not part of my everyday vocabulary. Alternatively, I used words like trauma, wounds, broken and anything fear-based, these words were my common vocabulary, that does not normalize them however. I then heard someone say, words have vibrations, like within the word **spell**ing, see them as loosely casting spells as you use them. This was the beginning of my journey. I started paying close attention to my word choices, a high self-monitor of what I was articulating to my outside and inner world. Words have meaning. Then I took it a step further by challenging the idea that sticks and stones can break my bones, but words will never hurt me. Words do hurt. I always heard that words can never hurt me, but they do and they did, in addition, words I speak to my inner self hurt equally, if not more. I began to live more aware of words and the feelings behind them, this became a very visceral experience. I felt the words from others, and I felt the words from me. So much of what I had allowed myself to say and hear was rooted in shame, guilt and very low feelings of self-worth. I am now in an empowering state of knowing I give meaning to the neutrality of the words I hear, and for all of us, this journey is very personal. Pivoting from things that no longer serve me is the leveling up experience I have always desired.

For personal reasons, I didn't have any desire to go to a therapist, I was worried this would give momentum to the problem which was simply a perspective I was choosing to believe. In hindsight, there are big parts of me that wish I had gone to a therapist but also was medicated. I chose other avenues for my emotional wellness that ultimately have served me... journaling became a conduit for healing, along with daily exercise.

Then during the pandemic and the frenzy of so many emotions experienced by all, I heard someone on the television ask, "Are you quieting your mind at least once a day?" For me, the answer was a hard no. I prided myself on being a fast-paced woman on the go, a single mom who could do it all, one that had created the mirage that she had it altogether. Quieting my mind was so easy as a child but now would feel so complex as an adult. I then also realized that meditation would mean dealing with my inner shit, being alone with my demons, and this wasn't for me. I then came to the realization that meditation could be enlightening when I asked myself, what if in peace I receive? This is a WHAT IF question for me that I felt compelled to explore and shine a flashlight of conscious awareness upon.

Practice, meditation takes practice. I had to tell myself this in the beginning as I struggled to quiet my mind for fifteen minutes daily.

When I did achieve the state of nothingness, this is when I began to experience the same visual imagery I did as a child. These moments would offer life-changing perspectives around my activated topics where I had split energy. Split energy feels like one foot on the dock, and one foot on the boat... one big, I want this BUT... am I worthy of it? And... do these amazing things really happen to a person like me? Am I being selfish with my manifestations? ALL THE THINGS. I realize now, however, when I meditate, I am in touch with my inner being, and she is very entertaining, very visual, has an extremely amusing imagination, and loves to tap into memories that, in my human head, have been long forgotten. My inner being also loves to swear, needless to say, this book is full of profanities. My meditative practice has given me the backstory on my love for the F WORD as my inner being finds swearing to be cathartic.

For those that are uncomfortable with swearing, according to a scientific study from Marist College in NY, intelligent people use more curse words. And guess what? Curse word fluency was found to be connected to traits of neuroticism and openness. I completely accept the openness aspect. Fuck yes! As I embrace my inner genius, there are often cuss words that enhance the journey.

A recent study published in *Frontiers in Psychology* found that repeating the "F" word during an ice water experiment increased subjects' tolerance and threshold for pain. Trust me when I say I am personally open to a study that concludes swearing can boost the threshold for pain.

So here we are, WE ARE SAYING FUCK YES to our LIVES as we desire them to be!

So be open, allow for openness as you read this.

YOU ARE THE ARCHITECT, you are the creator.

Why do I remind you of this? During this time, you may find yourself distracted by life's to-do list, the needs of others, everyday happenings, etc. I invite you to make the decision that you are reserving and preserving space for you. Simply decide. I did, and now I have stepped into my power. To be completely cliche, you cannot pour from an empty cup into a life meant to be a beautiful dream and not a nightmare.

The days of you outsourcing your energy are behind you as you embrace resourcing your energy from within.

PROGRAM TO REPROGRAM, this is not meant to be a page turner, but a journey full of guideposts towards your quantum self, you are possibly one perspective shift from changing your life. With the clients I work with, I strongly believe that it takes consistent guidance sessions to experience change, so I am sharing my own 30 day journey with the purest intention that you experience seismic shifts as well.

I am officially welcoming you to my visual journey…

It wasn't until recently that I realized that I have always been quantum leaping since I was a child, especially when my parents argued. I would imagine myself away in a safer place, I would put myself inside my blanket fort, and I would feel the comfort of being inside a safer dwelling, I would see myself staying strong, I would see and hear only things that brought me feelings of comfort. I didn't know then, but I know now that I was transmuting my energy from my current reality using the power of my imagination, and it was effective.

Having also grown up in poverty, I remember my teacher asking for us to bring $2.00 for field trip money, and my mom not having it. But I would decide to find it. I would go through every drawer, every bit of the Chevelle my mom drove, every piece of dirty laundry, and I would go to school with the $2.00 in a plastic baggy. I would be proud to be able to pay my own way, but inside me, there is exhaustion and shame. The dark truth of how I had to make that moment happen existed within me. I would continue that throughout my adult life by doing anything and everything to paint the picture that the money was always there, when in all honesty, I was practicing the old paradigm of working my ass off for it. I was ready for the new paradigm, where money comes to one easily and readily, where there is nothing to fix, solve or figure out. I was finally ready to rewrite my story choosing a narrative based on life feeling effortless. Again, this is where meditation came in. Life is meant for joy, not shame, effort, and exhaustion.

All along, even as a teenager, I discovered that quieting my mind holds the key to my calibration portal. In silence, I unlock my blocks. I can remember when I was sixteen and it was time to get my driver's license. I had friends who read the driver's manual, and they were ready for the test. Not me, I had to drive the car, read the book, talk about driving, see the roads, and truly embody the state of mind necessary to pass the test and be a safe driver. This is how I would also describe my downloads, going for a test drive, paying attention to the signs, until I reach my destination of feeling better. My inner being as my co-pilot, my spirit team protecting me, and the Universe providing for me in this vehicle we call the human experience.

Prior to the pandemic, I was at a winery with a group of friends, and there was a traveling tarot card reader giving readings. My friend told her she simply wanted to pull one card, and the card she pulled read, "MENTAL STILLNESS," with beautiful imagery of a woman surrounded by nature. These words stuck with me. It was me that was meant to see those words that evening, I knew my inner being wanted to make damn sure I allowed for mental stillness in my life, and this meant meditating. This was my calling to not only heal myself but to also heal others. This idea was reinforced at the beginning of the pandemic. There were barriers to getting a therapist, and even my family practitioner was booked out.

I knew it was time to refine and truly begin my healing journey with meditation.

I began this section with a quote from William James, an American philosopher, historian, and psychologist whose work included The James-Lange theory of emotion proposes that an event triggers a physiological reaction, which we then interpret. In accordance with this theory, emotions are caused by our interpretations of these physiological reactions. Through meditation I have been given the gift of interpreting my emotions through a higher consciousness where there is no judgment, only guidance through an up-leveled state of being. My emotions are my internal Global Positioning System, they guide towards my desires and reroute me when I am lost or off track.

As a result of all of what I just shared, this reading experience is a feeling journey, feel my words as you read them, give yourself permission to live outside of your self-inflicted limitations.

"Most of the shadows of this life are caused by our standing in our own sunshine."

— Ralph Waldo Emerson

Releasing Resistance Explained

I can only teach what I know, and what I know and believe in, is the power of the imagination. When it comes to visualization combined with one's imagination, our nervous system regulation plays a primary role in altering and bettering our somatic states allowing for personal expansion. During periods of chronic high stress, our bodies release stress hormones like adrenaline and cortisol, resulting in a multitude of health problems such as chronic pain, anxiety, and inflammation. The vagus nerve system, however, acts to counterbalance trauma responses by triggering relaxation sensations and by stimulating it we can receive powerful health benefits. One can stimulate the vagus nerve through deep breathing, meditation and visualization. Through my own learnings and life experiences, I believe that when you have memories that are creating limiting beliefs or abundance blocks, you can use imagination to reframe your perceptions. Similar to software program updates, we have the power to update our neurological activity, and we know that neurons that fire together, wire together. Our upgraded rewirings enhance our personal vibration making alignment more easily accessible.

A new brain imaging study led by University of Colorado Boulder and Icahn School of Medicine researchers suggests that imagination can be a powerful tool in helping people with fear and anxiety-related disorders overcome them. "This research confirms that imagination is a neurological reality that can impact our brains and bodies in ways that matter for our wellbeing," said Tor Wager, director of the Cognitive and Affective Neuroscience Laboratory at CU Boulder and co-senior author of the paper, published in the journal *Neuron*. One of the researchers suggests, "A lot of people assume that the way to reduce fear or negative emotion is to imagine something good. In fact, what might be more effective is exactly the opposite: imagining the threat, but without the negative consequences," said Wager. Wager also advises to pay attention to what you imagine by suggesting people to "Manage your imagination and what you permit yourself to imagine. You can use imagination constructively to shape what your brain learns from experience." [1]

If we take into account noteworthy personal accounts, it is worthwhile to shine a spotlight on Nikola Tesla and Thomas Edison.

Tesla imagined his work in great detail and that allowed him to save vast amounts of time, money and effort in designing and creating his machines. Tesla once stated, "I soon discovered that my best comfort was attained if I simply went on in my vision further and further, getting new impressions all the time, and so I began to travel; of course, in my mind. Every night (and sometimes during the day), when alone, I would start on my journeys – see new places, cities and countries; live there, meet people and make friendships and acquaintances...I could picture them all as real in my mind... I do not rush into actual work. When I get an idea, I start at once building it up in my imagination. I change the construction, make improvements and operate the device in my mind. It is absolutely immaterial to me whether I run my turbine in thought or test it in my shop."

Thomas Edison was famously opposed to sleeping, he thought sleep was a waste of time. In an 1889 interview published in *Scientific American*, the inventor claimed to have napped while holding a ball in each hand, and as he fell asleep, the ball would fall to the floor and wake him. This way he could remember the sorts of thoughts that come to us as we are nodding off, this is a practice similar to my own. I set an intention to feel better while activating my negative emotions, and then allow for my meditative state to guide me through a process focused on the emotion I would rather feel. When I am done meditating, I journal my visualizations and downloads.

To support this further, a study published recently in *Science Advances* reports that we have a brief period of creative insight in the semi lucid state that occurs just as we begin to drift into sleep, a sleep phase called N1, or non-rapid-eye-movement sleep stage 1. The findings imply that if we can harness that perceptible smog between sleep and wakefulness, known as a hypnagogic state, we might recall our ideas more readily. For me, this state of being allows me to find my flow, facilitate healing and achieve a higher state of consciousness. My intention for this book is for you to see the powerful marriage between science and the mind and how you can navigate your own healing, your own states of feeling better, by harnessing and calibrating your emotions during a meditative state. Whether it be an individual escapade or guided by a life coach or break-through specialist, a life where you fine tune your vibration leads to beautiful manifestations. Putting all science and data aside, there is undoubtedly a powerhouse within all of us when we activate our imagination during a meditative state.

On a deeply personal level, I have discovered all perspectives are fueled by emotions whether negative or positive, and by having a daily practice devoted to soul guidance through meditation, one can begin to release resistance. The reverse engineering process began for me when I realized I had to offer myself a reality check because I was not seeing all that I was calling in coming to fruition. Knowing manifestation is a feeling journey, I began to ask myself to what extent I was **resisting** love, abundance and freedom. I now live very aware of when energetically for me, there exists resistance.

Primarily, resistance is a feeling, thought, emotion, or behavior, either conscious or unconscious, in the form of limiting beliefs and abundance blocks. We are offered so many manifesting techniques like saying positive affirmations, journaling, and grounding. But in the end, stepping into the vibrational vicinity of one's desires is a journey towards releasing resistance. My origin story towards releasing resistance was birthed by getting very honest with myself. Through total accountability as a powerful creator, I begin a journey of personal exploration towards my limiting thoughts and beliefs especially at all levels of my being. As I continued to clear and let go of self-judgment and doubt through meditation and my imagination, I felt more authentically open to the life I desired. Your manifestations are not about what you want but who you are, there exists evidence everywhere in your life of what you are thinking, feeling and believing. Embrace the idea that all is well, and our lives are as good as we allow them to be. Allow alignment to be your priority and prepare yourself to release and receive through the power of now, meditation, appreciation, vibrational alignment, trust, and of course, your imagination.

---

1. Science Daily, 2018. *Your brain on imagination: It's a lot like reality, study shows.* From https://www.sciencedaily.com/releases/2018/12/181210144943.htm#:~:text=Previous%20research%20has%20shown%20that,regions%20related%20to%20the%20fingers

"Imagination is the beginning of creation. You imagine what you desire, you will what you imagine and at last you create what you will."

— George Bernard Shaw

Hello, Higher Self, Nice to Meet You

"The Universe does not know whether the vibration that you're offering is because of something you're observing or something you're remembering or something that you are imagining. It just receives the vibration and answers it with things that match it."

— Abraham Hicks

Have you met your higher self? Your higher self is your all good, all knowing, all powerful self. A belief is a thought we hold to be true, and is often based on how we interpret past experiences. My anxious self remembers the pain, the hostility, and the uncertainty of my formative years. My higher self shows up only through pureness and infinite love for where I have been, where I am, and where I am going.

Whether or not you are just now embarking on your spiritual journey, it is worth exploring that a person is much more than a mind and body, we also have a spiritual consciousness.

I believe in the power of the conscious, unconscious and higher conscious mind. As I have been taught, the conscious mind holds space for analysis. The unconscious mind is our storage unit of all memories and emotions. Our higher conscious mind houses our intuition, knowingness, and a connection with something beyond us as human beings. It is important to note that we are never separate from the SOURCE ENERGY from the Universe.

So many of us are guilty of keeping the door wide open to our older self, when we have the ability to open the door wide open to our new, more enlightened self. I believe your higher self and your older self can co-design a beautiful life for anyone. One of my primary passions is facilitating clients towards tapping into their higher selves. Many people accept the idea of their higher consciousness and higher self. There are those that may need proof of its existence, concrete evidence. For someone like myself, I have a strong connection that I heavily rely on, trust and connect with on a daily basis. By now meditating, exercising, and journaling I maintain an open valve of communication from my higher conscious mind to my unconscious mind to my conscious mind. This spiritual loop serves me on my journey. I have a very strong sense of intuition, I know my soul's purpose, I am tuned into answers from the divine, I am in more control of my emotions, my relationships are authentic, and my life feels less lonely.

I use the following from Accessing Higher Wisdom Technique By Catherine Warner – 2012.

Lay on the floor or in any comfortable position, feel completely relaxed, warm, and supported. Allow the slight noise of the beating of drums to be heard.

Now I want you to imagine that you are floating upwards, up out of the house. You can see the roof of the house and the tops of the trees around us. Up higher and you can feel a light mist on your face and it feels nice. Your body is so relaxed and comfortable, and your mind is out here in the sky, you might hear some night birds, and you keep rising higher and higher.

As you continue to rise you notice there are stars around you and it's very beautiful. You feel awed by this closest relationship to the heavens. And as you look around at the bright stars, you feel a powerful energy moving through you, it is like the whole Universe is surrounding you with love and wisdom. As you take a deep breath, you realize that all the answers you could ever need are right here in this beautiful starlight, and you can access this energy any time you are confused or in doubt.

Take a moment to breathe deeply and fill yourself with this new and wonderful energy. Now let's bring this energy down into your body, and know that you now have all the answers you are looking for. Down now, you see the tops of the trees and feel a fine cool mist on your face. Down through the roof, and feel your body. Feel your feet, and your hands, and when you're ready, open your eyes.

I then add my own flair by asking the client to now think of a time they felt amazing. What were you doing? What were you saying, what were you wearing, how were you composing yourself?

But here is the most important aspect of the higher self journey, this is not a time to create as if you are two separate entities, but to alchemize the relationship by FEELING what your Higher Self is FEELING. This is a feeling journey and your HIGHER SELF will show up from a place of ease, joy, satisfaction, contentment with love and above.

Now place this version of you in front of orange square. Really stare and embody this version of you, allow this to be your higher self, the version 2.0 of you.

When we shift from 3D consciousness to 5th dimensional consciousness by deeply connecting to our inner truths, we step into our own sovereignty of peace and empowerment. This is where we emotionally upgrade and begin to live life from a higher level of consciousness.

As you respond to the questions at the end of each section, I encourage you to tap into your higher self's feelings and this will level up your journey. Ask yourself, how might my Higher Self feel and respond?

How to have your HIGHER SELF follow the GUIDE posts?

I am not a spiritual teacher but a spiritual being having a human experience that I share as an uplifter. If you are triggered while reading this, allow these emotions in, this simply means you have something to soothe. Together we will isolate the emotion(s) and calibrate it to a better feeling place from a state of higher consciousness. I live in appreciation of my triggers, they are a beautiful invitation for exploration and personal expansion. This is your RSVP, you are responding to an invitation towards better, welcome to the party. Life is meant for joy.

We will begin with topics that I believe may resonate at some level, this is me being raw and transparent with my healing. You will be offered questions to ask and answer as a safe place to reflect as you implement and facilitate your own personal growth. I encourage you to allow divine timing with the unfolding of this journey from a pace and place that feels safe. One truth I accept as fact is the idea that when we calibrate to higher emotions by shifting our energy, we become a vibrational match to our desires, and we open the valve to higher frequencies. I love knowing it feels good to feel good, and again, if you have time to feel like crap, you have time to feel good. We will end with some of my most powerful shifts experienced with my clients. I share these as evidence that all of us can be connected to our higher self, whether we are guided to that place by someone like me, or we are self-guided. Feel our oneness, feel our connectedness, I am so appreciative to be on this journey with you. The imagery you will see and feel comes from a place of unconditional love, again, feel and see the words as you read them. I welcome you with open arms.

Keep in mind, non-resistant thoughts, where there is flow, are so much easier than resistant thoughts, where there are blocks. Embrace your leveling up by knowing that when a desire exists within you, the desire then already exists in a parallel Universe. The Universe is beautifully co-creating and orchestrating events and people that allow your desires to come to fruition in your new reality. Here is our role; it is through the dissolution of our resistance, where we will enter the receiving mode. As a side note, if ever an image feels cryptic to me, as it does at times, I allow myself to sit with it for a moment, knowing that in darkness there is light. My inner voice will eventually shine brighter with a message from my higher source, I relax and allow.

I began with thirty-one, yes thirty-one personal hot topics, where I felt the most recent wobble. I see these hot topics as emotional blocks that are cooking inside me, inviting me to heal from within. My dominant negative emotions are invitations and so are yours, they are inviting us to explore their meaning from a place of curiosity. I chose recent topics that are impacting me because I have come to realize that my past was seeping into my present day-to-day conditions. Daily self-soothing is a priority, and I always grew up hearing it takes thirty days to form a new habit, and my highest desire is to habitually feel better, so thirty plus days it is. I also know that one calibration a day allows for integration of my new thoughts, feelings and emotions into my physical reality. My goal is not to muddy the waters with too much congestion from energetic shifts but to clear the waters making room for better. I invite you to also allow for integration as well as go through the pages written from my state of total connectedness to my inner being.

Be reflective and intentional with your reading journey.

According to Abraham Hicks, telling it like it is, will hold it like it is.

By going through the offered exercises, this is your opportunity to share a different narrative about your life. Resistance vs. Allowance; release resistance and allow yourself to tell a different story. Introduce yourself and the world to a upleveled vibrational version of you, by clearing resistance, as one who has cleared the air that you breathe. By ultimately changing the meaning you have attached to your experiences and to yourself, by allowing your contrast to serve you in personal expansion, your life's oxygen feels cleaner and more refreshing. This is your permission slip to vibe with the solutions, as opposed to the problems. Welcome to a world where you will be tapping into your internal resources as you go into your own consciousness and begin to nourish your soul from the inside out. For those that have a dimmed spiritual light, you attracted this book because you are ready to ease up the dimmer switch and allow more lightness in.

I go back to when I was an elementary teacher, and students who tested well were identified as TALENTED AND GIFTED. I became one who advocated that all students are talented and gifted, if we are going to be in the business of giving out labels, then all students are worthy of this label. It wasn't until I began my spiritual journey that I saw myself as one who is also TALENTED AND GIFTED, we all are. By choosing to look under your personal hood and priming the pump, you are choosing to live in awareness of your gifts as a whole. We all have unique talents and we all have gifts. To take it a step further, I am the fucking gift, and so are you. Repeat after me, "I am the fucking gift." Breathe this in and feel it.

I love knowing that all of us may be one energetic shift from changing our lives. I begin my imaginative journey by seeking the frequencies that are in alignment with the truth of who I am and I allow myself to release old energies and move into a new consciousness. I no longer desire for my story to be one of procrastination, limiting beliefs and self-sabotage. My imagination brilliantly worked for me as a child, and I allowed the perceived seriousness of adulthood to dissolve my healing imagery. I now offer a life phase themed by: THAT WAS THEN AND THIS IS NOW, allowing the imagination I had as a child to continue to heal me as an adult.

As for you, I encourage you to allow your energetics to transfer so effortlessly because you are ready and open to receiving. Feel the flow within each shift you experience. My outward guidance and imagery are simply facilitating your inward experience. Again, this is not an effort *none* experience, it is an effort *less* journey. When you connect to the lightness of spiritual guidance, you are giving yourself permission to let go of the things, the thoughts and the people that no longer serve you. This immersive reading journey is not meant to be binged, although we live knowing we can process so much information at a time because of our technological influences like the internet. This is one chapter at a time, and one day at a time reading experience. Allow the current to guide you by integrating your new state of being through ease, joy and flow. You and I are co-creating and celebrating together. You too are a Master of the Universe. After this experience, you will have brand new boundaries as you calibrate to the next level and embrace your power as a creator. Allow this to be a space and place where you completely revolutionize your entire existence. You are worth it and as co-creators we are expanding our receptive mode, which in turn attracts your desires in.

Reframe and Receive. I know by releasing resistance we put ourselves within the vibrational vicinity of our desires. All of us came here to discern through contrast, and to go in the direction of our own inner guidance. When we reframe our stories as a conscious creator, we are allowing for the embodiment of all we desire and making room for joyful excitement.

As the Universe writes through me, allow the words to be for you, metaphorically speaking. As I said earlier, not only do I recommend reading the words, but feeling them at the visceral level, embracing the imagery, knowing you are possibly only one perspective shift from changing your life. Together we are making our unknowns known, and by doing so, we are living on the leading edge where life feels limitless. *Beyond you*, that place where we are stepping out of our comfort zone and our new story begins through your higher self.

It is exhilarating to know that when we take the time to connect, we can channel our truths. This journey is not about coming to our senses, but feeling and seeing the sensations and allowing them to guide us. There is so much power in loving yourself enough to disrupt trauma's impact or the things that are weighing you down by exploring who you are without negative emotions.

We appropriately begin our open communication alongside the Universe with the topic of self-love. As the Law of Attraction suggests, like energies attract like energies and is based on the belief that positive or negative thoughts bring positive or negative experiences into a person's life. You put YOU in the Universe. Living aware of our *attraction point* by living aware of our dominant emotions, whether perceived as negative or positive, that characterize our various circumstances is an opportunity to level up. By making small or epic shifts every day, we can consciously facilitate thoughts and energy to attract our purest desires.

If we can allow for suffering, we can allow for healing. When we don't heal, what is unhealed continues to show up in our physical reality, and may even repeat itself.

YOUR LIMITING THOUGHTS are YOUR LIMITATIONS. Visualize.

Every word will guide you through the calibration portal towards your higher self, simply allow and be ready to be ready. I was ready, and if you are reading this book, you are ready as well.

This is your reminder that in our 3rd dimension on earth, we all have things to resolve. When you discover, embrace and release this stored energy you free up space for your divinity to come through. Our suffering can be the catalytic pathfinder leading us to personal healing and freedom. Allow for spiritual elasticity as we shift away from the illusory events of the world and embrace our inner world.

I have set an intention that all readers appreciate the structure of this book as it is written through a stream of consciousness...where the metaphors make it poetic and many of the words are merely decorous enhancements highlighting the ultimate divine downloads.

REPEAT AFTER ME: I am open and ready to release all that is no longer serving me. I am eager to acknowledge and take personal responsibility for my inner energy.

Let us begin by knowing that manifestation is a feeling journey.

"Whether you succeed or not is irrelevant, there is no such thing. Making your unknown known is the important thing, and keeping the unknown always beyond you."

— Georgia O'Keeffe

Landing in Love

Attraction Point to Ponder 1

I have been in a long term relationship for seven years. And to be honest, looking back, I have a habit of what feels like falling out of love around the 6 year mark. This is nothing personal towards the person I am with, this is simply a pattern of mine worth exploring.

Intellectually, I live very aware that even couples who have been together for any length of time may go their separate ways. This is where my confusion exists, why would I continuously and deliberately want to dissolve relationships I have invested so much time in? For me personally it never has to do with the lack of physical touch, lack of communication, trust, unresolved issues or boredom. It is not easy to accept or understand this, but going through breakups often has more to do with me and my bull shit than any particular relationship dynamics.

I have a strong tendency to notice when my relationships are heading south, and I have been very guilty for allowing them to do so. Self-sabotage at its finest. I am ready to own my relationship stories by shifting my patterns. With respect to my former lovers, I will keep the details to a minimum and place primary focus on me.

As I relax and think about the unfoldings around me, I realize I am falling out of love, or am I?

As I quiet my mind, the emotion is confusion, knowing my personal track record of fight or flight, primarily flight. The thought brings nausea and instant repulsion, I feel a heavy green blob, mass, energy within my stomach. I immediately want to feel better. The negativity behind this feeling is overwhelming. Immediately I am offered the image of a traffic light, red light on the bottom, yellow light in the middle, and green light on top. My ego shows me the red light, I hear, "STOP! Carry on in this human experience with the other human, there are too many unknowns with leaving." I want to throw up. My ego desires to keep me safe, that damn comfort zone, but I do not feel safe. Moving my thoughts upward, I see the YELLOW LIGHT, I hear, "Proceed with Caution." Again, this feels so fear-based. I move up to the GREEN LIGHT, and I hear loud and clear, "Green means GO!" This is the permission slip I have been waiting to hear and see. GO! I convince myself this suggestion to flee is coming from a place of unconditional love. This feels way too easy, I begin to feel better, I allow the green light to move over me, I remind myself to see beyond my perceived limitations. Yep, I can simply go. I deserve to have it all, there is a knowing to this. Feeling myself moving forward I see myself getting into a car like one I saw in the GREAT GATSBY movie, the car literally chugs along, I feel at peace with this, I am not ready to move at an overwhelming speed. I feel laughter, a roof down in a convertible feeling, it's breezy and freeing. I look up to see a street sign that reads ROMANTICIZE.

The car stops.

How can I romanticize my life if I am choosing to be alone? Cozy pajamas? Plush slippers? Lit candles? Taking my own self out to dinner?

I felt the humanness behind these responses.

The fear of being alone still was lingering, it was time to allow the answers to come in from my higher self and not my fear-based ego.

I am then offered a reminder, I am a spiritual being having a human experience.

With this reminder, I feel the knowing, the knowing that I am never alone, I am never alone. None of us are ever *really alone.*

There is Source energy all around me, I am and have God, and my inner being loves me unconditionally.

This was the green light, this is the permission slip; I can go forward with no fear of being alone; I have a spiritual army that surrounds me at all times.

Maybe just knowing I can always leave, always just go, or simply exit is enough for me. It doesn't mean I have to do so, but there is a feeling of safety knowing the option is there.

I am reminded my quantum self is always thriving and appreciates personal expansion, my human self is simply surviving by stopping at the red light without examining why I sabotage relationships. I realized the red light was actually a symbol telling me to stop and reflect.

I internalize this idea of being reflective by envisioning myself having a place at a dining table, sitting alone. Whether there are candles lit, food served, perfect lighting, why do I desire to sit alone with myself, where I don't even look happy, then have someone sit with me in a long term commitment?

Feeling the confusion still, the ultimate download I receive is this:

When you fall out of love with yourself, it allows you to easily mirror the feeling of falling out of love with others.

Had I fallen out of love with myself? Possibly. At times, I feel like I have lost myself in motherhood, work and relationships.

I am immediately slapped with the realization that none of this is actually about falling out of love with my partner, none of this is actually about being alone... this journey is about being in love with myself. I appreciated the reassurances, but ultimately, I needed to be reminded of the power of self-love within a relationship.

The divine download: FALL IN LOVE WITH YOURSELF FIRST and continue to land in love with yourself in all aspects of your life. Fall and land.

I could feel the power in embracing self-love and how it could change my deliberate course of my relationships.

I am responsible for my own happiness. If I am going to show up as an equal, I have to first think about how I am going to define myself from a place of love for me then a partner.

Self-love is a vital *part* of being in a *part*nership.

Validate from within first, then give yourself approval to change your mind at any time from a place of self-love.

So many allow themselves to get lost in love with another person, and this download about partnerships is a solid recommendation to not get lost in love with yourself.

Allow self-love to be an incremental journey, tune into things daily that allow you to stay in alignment with what brings you personal happiness.

If you want a long-term relationship with someone, maintain a long term commitment to yourself.

When you say I love you to someone, make sure you can also say I LOVE ME to yourself.

Each day, ask yourself, "How can I give myself a little more love?"

Ultimately, self-love is the receiving and allowing mode of love from another.

This *a-ha* feels amazing.

Looking back, instead of going inward, I was always solving relationship turmoil by outwardly breaking up with whoever I was with. My OPTIMUM personal agreement is to allow ways to fall in love with me again. I begin to allow in versions of me that I am in love with, like who I am when I am cooking, who I am as an uplifter, and who I am as a mom. I set an intention to embody the versions of me that I am madly in love with and have my own little love affair with myself.

I envision myself standing up at the same dining table again and I offer a toast, I toast myself and my spirit team. I confidently raise a glass and thank all of us for allowing in the reminder that I am never alone. I appreciate choosing to thrive rather than to just survive while in a relationship, and to understand loving another for any length of time is to begin by loving and staying in love with myself.

I stand there embracing my quantum self and know the Universe always provides as I again allow for the intention to not only fall in love with myself all over, but to land in love with myself and stay there.

I close this meditation knowing the word *partnership* so differently. I now see how self-love is the primary *part* of the relationship's success. Self-love is the part in a partnership that must come first.

1. If you sabotage relationships, explore your pattern and discover why this may be.
2. What does self-love mean to you, and how can you allow more of it for yourself? What is actual evidence of your degree of self-love within your relationships? Do you think self-love is selfless? Explain from your Higher Self's perspective.
3. Ask yourself what permission slip can you give yourself in order to choose relationship happiness from a place of self-love. Are you open to the idea that loving yourself more can allow you to love others more?
4. What are ways you can truly fall in love with yourself, where you fall and land in a place of completely appreciating the essence of your entire being, ideally from your Higher Self? What would a true love affair with yourself look and feel like?
5. What toast can you offer yourself and your spirit team from a place of total appreciation?

Growth through Crisis

Attraction Point to Ponder 2

In my early twenties, I worked for a non-profit organization. I cannot begin to describe in words the level of intensity as we served primarily low-income families. Sometimes there were board decisions made that the staff did not agree with, there were children not having their basic needs met, there were families longing for more help than we could offer, and as always, we had budgetary uncertainties. When our little non-profit world felt like it was turned upside down, our director would reassure all of us with these words, "There is growth through crisis." I once asked him to elaborate as to how one might actually experience growth through crisis, and he replied, "Be solution-oriented and not problem-focused." These words resonated with me then, and their meaning has evolved as I have evolved.

In recent years, our world has been faced with a trauma tsunami as we were all hit with the fierce and high waves of a global pandemic, economic uncertainties, unexplainable violence, and now a war in Europe.

I have some in my circle that say, "I simply don't watch the news so it doesn't impact me." Others tell me when they watch the news they get mad. No judgment from me either way, but I do watch the news. I do so with a high level of discernment as I see the news as a means to feel connected to the world around me. My choice and typically I am able to watch current events and stay in my steady state.

With the recent events in the world, I am reminded to live in the energy of the solution and not the problem, but today that does not feel like enough. This is a humanitarian crisis, and anything that feels problematic to my life now feels minuscule to what those innocent civilians are facing. So here I sit, torn. I am tired today because I didn't sleep well last night, but how can I complain when it wasn't the sounds of missile explosions and sirens that kept me awake. I have food, safety, and a home. I am in my home country and not a refugee. I have all my creature comforts. My son is at college and not at war. My daughter is home with me.

I ask myself, how do I validate my perceived individual problems that now feel so invalid compared to what others are going through?

As I feel the emotions of fear and some helplessness activated within me, I am aware that I am feeling like I am not doing enough for those fighting for their lives, their country and their freedom.

Slowing down my mind, I allow myself to feel like I am sitting at the ocean. This is a very tactile experience as I feel the wind, smell the ocean breeze, feel the sound of calm waves crashing, rub my feet in the sand, and see the beauty of the vastness. I can feel my breathing slowing down as there is no tsunami in sight.

I am reminded of the power of grounding one's self daily.

I then see myself along the shoreline holding a bucket and a spoon.

I can recall my personal investor discussing a financial situation that called for money to be put down, and he told me that I can stand waiting for the wave of cash coming my way with either a spoon or a bucket. My item of choice would depend on how much I invested, a larger investment meant I would be standing with the bucket expecting a large financial windfall, and a spoon meant I should expect a far less amount in return. This moment, however, was not about financials, it was about feelings.

I thought about all of the feelings the ocean offers to me from a place of ease, joy and flow. Then I thought about a huge fear I have of the ocean and this was the idea of swimming in it.

Which item am I going to fill fear with, the spoon or the bucket? Undoubtedly in my mind, I was going to fill the bucket with water from a place of unconditional love and higher level emotions. The spoon would get a very little amount to represent my fear.

Faith over fear. Trust. Surrender.

I fill the bucket to the very brim with feelings of love and above, and I feel my steadiness as I don't allow any of the water to spill over. I wanted to leave very little room, if any, for fear. There are feelings of being in control of my emotions at this moment and this feels reassuring.

The fear is there, but seeing it in a spoon makes it feel small. I decide to allow the spoonful of fear to go into the bucket, knowing my love and above emotions will dominate. I begin to feel better as I embrace that I am my own bucket-filler, as a powerful creator, I can allow higher emotions to fill me up.

As the meditation continues, I then see myself turn around, and similar to an amusement park in Santa Cruz, CA. I see a roller coaster right on the beach.

This was more than a cliche moment where I already knew that life has its ups and downs, or life is like a roller coaster, not a merry-go-round. There was more to this. I see myself getting on the roller coaster with a group of strangers, we are buckled in by someone we don't know, and we ride the ride together. With people I have never met, I am sharing fear, excitement, and rattling coaster carts.

This imagery allows me to be reacquainted with the idea that life has emotional highs and lows...there are often good times alternating with really difficult times. There are moments when we want to scream and there are moments when we are simply enjoying the ride.

My mind then goes back to the idea that I am sharing my emotions, my trust, and my faith in a roller coaster's safety with complete and total strangers. When we stand in line for a roller coaster, ideally, we wait and board with trust, and the thrill of it all puts our fears at bay and we show up with an expression of trust that goes beyond the conscious mind.

We show up with faith.

During any moment, even when there is a humanitarian crisis, we need to show up not from a frequency of fear but from a frequency of faith.

This beautiful download was then received: *We are powerful creators, this is not the time to stop creating because we are fearful; we need to keep creating from a place of love, peace and faith.*

Faith over fear. Trust. Surrender.

The message is consistent.

With this message I embrace the power of collective consciousness.

As a Social Work major in college, I am reminded of learning about founding sociologist Émile Durkheim. He developed this concept of collective consciousness to explain how unique individuals are bound together into units like society and social groups. Collective consciousness is something "common to the whole of society," as Durkheim describes. It is a social condition, not an individual one, and through collective consciousness we pass down values, beliefs, and traditions through generations.

Spiritually, I view collective consciousness as promoting solidarity by binding people through their shared practices, beliefs, and values. And as I think of war, I trust and surrender that the majority of the collective is bound by protecting our freedoms.

Through our collective consciousness, where society as a whole is made up of individual frequencies, I believe we can save lives. We have to be proactive and not reactive. Again, we have to be solution-oriented and not problem-focused.

I then begin to think about the vision board I create with pure intentions at the beginning of every new year. With a heavy heart, I realize that all of my desires are created for me as an individual. My dream house, my dream car, my dream vacation, and at this moment that all feels blah and nonsensical. I am reminded how the power of visualization can be used not only to simply impact my individual journey but through our collective journey. It feels better to create not just for me, but from me for the entire collective. I envision others inspired to raise their personal vibration with a knowingness that together we can raise the frequency felt by all.

As one of my favorite mentors used to say, "Rising waters lift all boats."

When we identify and connect with the masses, we never leave anyone behind... we in turn move forward for all of humanity through the frequency of our individual vibrations.

I close this meditation, knowing it is now more important than ever to show up from a place of love and trust, this is not the time to cower down to our fears and play small. By connecting to our divinity within, by soothing even our smallest individual problems, we may save a life. Knowing that this life's ride is often shared with total strangers, without even directly knowing one another, our interdependence is vital. We can share faith over fear when it comes to our safety and our freedoms, starting with individuals like me. I am not directly in war, so accessing a higher state may be easier than one who is literally on the front lines.

Then I hear this and I know it can be heard only by those ready for its message:

Times of uneasiness in the world are not the times for an emotional rollercoaster relationship with your personal vibration.

For those that can, this is the time to fill your bucket with the emotional highs full of connection, fulfillment, and love, whereas feeling the lows of disconnect and fear simply get the spoon.

Stay steady for universal steadiness.

Keep showing up, not only for yourself, but for our entire world.

There is growth through crisis, even during a global crisis.

1. Are you able to watch or hear current events and stay in a steady state? When you hear local or world news that is unsettling, how do you typically feel and react? How would your higher self feel and react when presented with the same news?

2. Do you find yourself in the energy of the solution more often or in the energy of the problem? Describe a current situation where you could allow for more emphasis on the solution. Be proactive, not reactive, detach from any specific outcome, and go general by feeling what this solution would feel like.

3. What frequency can you tap into easily and readily and emit that may lift the vibration of the entire collective simply by starting at the individual level? What emotions can you fill your bucket with, leaving very little room for your fears? Explore various areas of your life where fear may be dominating and allow yourself to tap into feelings of faith and trust.

4. What are some daily practices that can allow you to navigate through the emotional highs and lows of life so you are tending to your personal vibration daily? Grounding? Pivoting? Pivoting can be a way of momentarily getting off a topic that is causing your stress. Napping?

5. Are you open to the idea that the frequencies we emit as individuals can make a difference in the lives of others? Explore this with depth.

Feathering Your Nest

Attraction Point to Ponder 3

In a very short time, I will be an empty nester; both of my children will be over eighteen and living away from home in college. I can recall learning about the empty nest syndrome, it is most common in the primary care provider and is typically the grief experienced when the children move out of the home. I have to admit that there are bits that excite me, like the toilet lid being closed, the remote being where I left it, the cupboards having food longer, and there being less laundry. At this very moment, however, I think of these listed changes, and I still feel a sense of sadness.

When my children were young, someone gifted me a printed version of the poem, WET OATMEAL KISSES, and I used a magnet to place it on the fridge:

Wet Oatmeal Kisses by Erma Bombeck

The baby is teething-the children are fighting. My husband just called and said to eat dinner without him. Okay, one of these days you'll shout: "Why don't you grow up and act your age!" And they will, or, "You guys get outside and

> find yourselves something to do...and don't slam the
> door!" *...and they won't.*
> *You'll straighten up their rooms neat and tidy...bumper
> stickers discarded...spreads tucked and smooth... toys
> displayed on the shelves... hangars in the closet... animals
> caged, and you'll say out loud:* "Now I want it to stay that
> way!" *And it will... You'll prepare a perfect dinner with a
> salad that hasn't been picked to death and a cake with no
> finger traces in it and you'll say,* "Now there's a meal for
> a company." *And you'll eat it alone.*
> *You'll say,* "I want complete privacy on the phone. No
> dancing around, no pantomimes, no demolition
> crews. Silence! Do you hear?" *...and you'll have it. No
> more plastic tablecloths stained with spaghetti, no more
> anxious nights under a vaporizer tent, no more dandelion
> bouquets, no more iron-on patches, knotted shoestrings, or
> tight moots.*
> *Imagine, a lipstick with a point, no babysitter for New Year's
> Eve, washing clothes only once a week, no P.T.A. meetings,
> carpools, blaring radios, Christmas presents out of tooth-
> picks and paste. No more "Wet Oatmeal Kisses". No more
> tooth fairy giggles in the dark or knees to heal.*
> *Only a voice crying...* "Why don't you grow up?" *...and the
> silence echoing...* "I did."

The poem reads so differently now than it did THEN. Then I was exhausted and knee deep in sleepless nights, now I am more rested but sleepless because of different reasons. When I think of my children leaving the nest, I find my human self worrying about what if they fall, I then allow my higher self brilliantly respond with, but what if they fly? But still, there exists sadness.

Recently, I keep rereading the last line of the poem: **Only a voice crying...** *"Why don't you grow up?"...and the silence echoing... "I did."*

Not long ago, I was driving in the car with my daughter and I was prob-ably being annoyingly reflective with her. I asked her this question,

"Would you rather have had your nest completely feathered, or have the nest you grew up in to be a little unfeathered?" Her response surprised me. Without any hesitation, she immediately stated, "I would rather feather my own nest than have someone else feather it for me, and to take it a step further… I am the fucking feathered nest."

Needless to say, I have had many proud mom moments, and well, this was indeed one of them. My mind told me she is going to be just fine adulting, my heart still wants to protect her even though I know she is as ready as she can be.

Just a few days later, she came home and I was in a heated discussion about a stressful situation with my partner. Right when she walked in the door, she asked, "Is everything ok?" I instinctively responded, "Absolutely, no worries."

I just fucking gaslit my own seventeen year old daughter. Not ok. The last thing I want is to diminish her intuition that is telling her that something is wrong. I want her to know when she is in a compromising situation and trust her inner guidance system, and not doubt it. I later apologized and validated her intuitiveness…I want her to have situational awareness and trust her gut instincts.

I was now sitting with all of the times I steered her away from her own accurate emotional guidance. With the idea that I was actually protecting her, I was actually manipulating her so she would feel safe. Some may argue that we should protect our children from stress, and this is true. But what we shouldn't do is extinguish their intuitive senses designed to help them sense trouble. I don't want either of my children doubting their ability to read a room or, God forbid, an abusive relationship they may be entering.

So here I stand at the precipice of the empty nest, and I can feel all of the scattered energy. At one point, I was a young woman giving birth to my children, and now I am giving birth to mixed emotions: sadness, regret, guilt. I was hatching emotions that were being conceived from a very low vibrational state.

As I soothe my mind in meditation, I almost immediately see Dorothy from WIZARD OF OZ on the yellow brick road, and initially I think of one's desire to find the way back home to our real self, one step at a time. Then I think about how the pathways of our adult life are not paved in gold. Intellectually, I do not want my children to think this, but emotionally I do. I think about how being overprotective can actually be a form of manipulation, they are here for growth and expansion and I need to get out of the way. It is just hard to let go.

The quote from Glinda, the good witch, came to mind, "You always had the power, my dear, you just had to learn it for yourself." I can feel the split energy in how this quote resonates with me now as it is applied to my son and daughter versus just me. Yes, I know my kids have always had the power, and they will learn how to use it on their own, but dammit, I want them to know they will always have me.

My own mortality is inevitable, which in itself feels heavy, but while I am in this physical reality and for all of eternity, I know being their mom is my primary soulmate experience.

I find myself hearing the words of that poem again and again. **Only a voice crying... *"Why don't you grow up?"*...and the silence echoing... *"I did."***

It is at this point, I realize I have regrets, this is my dominant negative emotion, so I isolate this emotion and ask for guidance towards feeling better.

I feel the tears and my stomach is achy.

Within moments, I am offered a memory of my children and I holding hands walking down the sidewalk of our old neighborhood. We see our shadows ahead of us. My shadow is in the middle, and I am holding the hand of my son on my right, and my daughter on my left. I recall my daughter innocently asking me, "If I step on someone's shadow, will it hurt the person?" I reassured her with a very loving, "They will not feel it." My son then asked, "If I don't like my shadow following me, how do I get rid of it?" I am sure I could have offered him a scientific explanation, or maybe one from a photographer's perspective, but at that moment I simply said, "You can turn your back to a different angle until it disappears, or you can go into a shady area." Both of them seemed satisfied with the responses I offered.

But now the conversation about shadows would be entirely different with them as adults. I now begin thinking about shadow work. Shadow work is often referred to as the parts of ourselves we may try to keep hidden, yet they still may be casting shade on our feelings. There are many experts that believe, whether through a therapist or on your own, there's a way to tap into the darkness of the shade to deepen personal growth. Some benefits include healing generational trauma, feeling whole, and being emotionally healthy.

Through my own realizations, I am having this new awareness that my shadows are not shade at all... they are transformative and move me towards the light. I don't want to turn my back on my life's shadows, I want to see them before me and allow them to be transformative. I feel the energetic shift as I move from seeing shadow work as actually being light work. Just like when we were on that walk that day, there is nothing to fear in facing our shadows in front of us, because they have been with us all along.

My highest desire is for my family to live with self-awareness by being open to casting light on the uncomfortable in order to feel more comfortable. I begin to think about how our individual lives are all a spiritual journey, one does not enter this life suddenly and magically when becoming an adult. We are eternal beings. Shadow work, light work, transformative work, is acknowledging the value of your inner turmoil. When you acknowledge the shade of your emotions, you are then open to exploring what gives you light through personal expansion.

Just me and my shadows. Just my children and their individual shadows. We are all on our own journeys.

I feel myself shifting from regret to satisfaction in knowing I have modeled how to show up as our authentic selves to both my children. We have always walked with our shadows, and whether or not I am holding their hands, I know they are both leaving the nest, knowing thoughts and emotions are reflected in their physical reality. This is not the empty nest phase, nor is it the emptiness phase, it is a full phase. I can live in full satisfaction knowing my children are empowered adults living very aware of being powerful creators. So yes, even with the wet oatmeal kisses of the past, and as we walked with our shadows together hand-in-hand, all of us, even you, have always had the power. When the outer world presents external circumstances that are out of our own control, we can find control within our inner world.

When we allow light, we feel lighter.

We simply have to learn our life's lessons for ourselves. Be your own feathered nest.

I come out of this meditation knowing there will always be a time space reality where the three of us are still holding hands like that day on our walk. No matter where we are in the world, we are eternally connected.

1. Looking back on your life, knowing what you know now, would you rather have had your nest feathered or unfeathered? Explain by offering details on how you allow your past to serve you.
2. Do you gaslight your loved ones? When they care so much to ask if you are indeed alright, do you answer honestly, or do you manipulate your response? Explore how you respond. Do you have authentic intentions with your responses?
3. What power have you learned for yourself that empowers you through the perceived difficult times? How can this power play a role in influencing better outcomes for you? What would be an exhilarating way for you to show the Universe you are ready to shine your light?
4. Are you open to seeing your shadow work as light work? How can you allow your past experiences, where there may be moments shaded by unhappiness, to be moments where you show the Universe you expanded as an individual?
5. If you are experiencing a change in your nest, whether it be a breakup, children moving out, divorce; how can you replace feelings of emptiness with feelings of fullness? Allow in full feelings of satisfaction by embracing relationship moments with others and even yourself that elevate your vibration.

From a Worrier to a Warrior

Attraction Point to Ponder 4

Today I am WORRIED about EVERYTHING. Full disclosure, I have always been a worrier. As a little girl, my mom told me that if I did not have something to worry about, I would create something to worry about. When I was pregnant with my firstborn, I remember even worrying that my son would be a worrier like his mother. Worries manifest themselves, trust me. When my son was in preschool, he was able to pick out a special book on his birthday and he selected THE WORRIED WALRUS by Richard Hefter. His preschool teacher told me that she could not think of a more fitting book for him. It was at that moment that I felt like my worried state was so extreme, it had actually crossed the placental barrier.

I even often remind myself that worrying is like praying for the unwanted but here I am still worrying.

I now believe that my son and I can break the cycle of generational worrying through meditation and reframing so I am committed to moments of peace daily.

Today is a day where I was actually excited for my full mind to feel mindful.

As I quieted my mind, a flashing rectangular sign like the word VACANCY took over, and immediately I wished it read NO VACANCY, like we don't need to feel worried because we are already so full of uplifting emotions. Ideally, the body's hotel policy would be: No shifts, no good news, no service! In fact, all of my worries in an ideal world have been 86ed. Not today though, the sign is now flashing WORRIES over and over and over. In my life, however, I have decided to no longer turn off my emotions, if that was the case, I would simply mentally unplug my sign and go on with my day, but deep down I know a negative energetic charge would eventually light the sign back up. My life now is one where I choose to energetically shift my emotions by tuning into higher states of being. My inner guidance system immediately desires to see the letters as a neon sign outside of the rectangle box, this feels better as I beautifully change the word WORRIES to Liz, this already feels better, this moment becomes about *me*. I find immediate ease in this, but my mind goes back to the rectangular structure of the sign. My mind sees a semi truck. Where is this going, I ask myself, but I follow my flow. No questions asked. I see the entire semi truck parked and facing a long yet welcoming road ahead. Going around the back, I notice the back is open, and the truck is empty, my smell senses are not activated, thank goodness. Not being able to smell the ignition fumes nor what was piled up behind the truck would make the kinesthetic experience I was about to have more pleasurable. I see piles and piles of shit and a big shovel. Immediately I realize the shit I see is the shitshow I have made out of my emotions today, but the Universe has handed me a shovel. Empowerment. I immediately felt empowered. I begin shoveling the shit into the back of the semi, each load representing a worry, or a memory that created a worry. I feel angelic empowerment, like a white glow around me giving new meaning to 6 foot distancing, the distancing is happening because I illuminate for all to see even from a distance. I am choosing to be seen, to be heard, and to show up from a state of total well-being while giving my emotions a colonic cleanse.

I shovel away the feelings of food insecurity I grew up with as a child, I shovel away worries about our world's current state of happenings, I shovel away my insecurities, I shovel away a weight comment made to me by a former lover, I shovel away what I think others think of me, and I shovel away a big pile of anxiety. I keep shoveling away all of the shit I have seen and heard.

I feel the shovel, I hear the scraping of the sidewalk, I embody my strength, and start shoveling the bull shit to the back of a welcoming semi, with a driver ready to drive them away. THE UNIVERSE ALWAYS PROVIDES, the empty semi is my conduit to a better feeling state.

I shovel until there is no more, I am not tired, I am energized, I have cleared away the negative emotions that have made me feel like I just had sex without even getting a kiss. The emotional booty calls are over, they only leave me feeling empty. My new emotional standards are now higher than ever. I know I am not spiritually bypassing anything at this moment. I am holding a shovel and moving the shit that feels so close to me through my worried state and disconnecting from it in terms of creating a healthy distance of my choice.

I stand there and watch the back of the truck come down, the worries are sealed away, and I assume a power stance with my fists to my hips. This is not a superhero pose, this is me taking charge of my anxious thoughts. Again, angelic empowerment. There I stand and there is a glow to me, there is a state of being that radiates from a place of wellness, there is me choosing to no longer play small. THERE IS ME on my team and I am the MVP. Suddenly my mind changes the letters in TEAM around, and I see ME AT, and I feel the following words, ME AT HAPPINESS, ME AT LOVE, ME AT HARMONY, ME AT INNER PEACE. With each breath, I feel these words within my DNA, within every cell of my being, and it is at that moment, I begin waving goodbye. The semi begins to drive away. ME AT FAREWELL to the worry clusterfuck that has constipated my emotional growth for too long.

This is my new baseline. This is where all decisions are made from, this is where all emotions start, this is where all thoughts begin, and this is where actions have their onset. My ME AT statements are my new starting points, I am consciously changing my point of attraction towards my desires and not away from them.

Suddenly disrupted by an image I feel my thoughts say, wait, what????
Why would my mind allow me to see a sign on the back that reads,
MAKES FREQUENT STOPS, no, no, and no. My highest desire is to keep
the semi going, no stops, having it move along the road with flow and
ease, carrying the shit that longer serves me far, far away. Then I
remember angelic empowerment. I am a powerful creator, my mind
simply chooses different words: CONTAINS TOXIC WASTE. This is not
a magical process, it is logical, it is a law, and so it is. I choose. I create. I
expect. I decide. It's done. The Art of Allowing. Worrying is a waste of my
imagination. Worrying is praying for the unwanted. I now welcome experiences and moments where I am triggered to mean I have something to
heal as opposed to something I need to worry about. I know and grasp the
power of my thoughts.

The semi continues down the road, CONTAINS TOXIC WASTE, is
written across the back, and for a little added fun, I have the license plate
read my favorite angelic number: 1111.

As I look around in the shit that is still lingering around me.... possibly
the missed piles, I think of compost. I know that composts break down
organic matter to create humus, a rich nutrient-filled material. Like
compost, my worries can become, when properly managed, fertile ground
to grow into life-giving thoughts.

I am my own intricate ecosystem.

My worry shitshow feels over.

For all of us. Decide.

When we are standing in shit, we are still standing in our power.

We are choosing to take inspired action. We are choosing for our minds to
be a valuable resource. We are choosing to revitalize our thoughts.

The toxic wasteland of life can be one where limiting beliefs and memories may close our receiving valve off, but we can allow for the colonic
cleanse of negative emotions to be our spiritual detox.

As I close out this visualization, I see my past from a state of empowerment, the rest of my day feeling energized, and my future from a place of
coding to lightness. I am free.

My negative emotions are not toxic wastes, nor am I choosing to permanently seal them off, I am simply getting a hold of them before they get a
hold of me. I can wave goodbye when necessary or I can hold the shovel,
or I can stand knee-deep in it all, no matter what, I am in control of my
connectivity to and the meaning I give to my worries.

Taking a deep breath and feeling the energetic shifts, I release what does
not serve me and I hear:

Be a warrior, not a worrier.

1. When do you feel most empowered? What does this state feel like within your body? How can you embody this state more often?
2. **Take a moment, and ask yourself this,** _"If the Universe handed you a shovel, one specifically designed to clean up your emotional shitshow, what memory, memories, or thoughts are amplifying your worries?"_ What are the worries you could shovel away from an empowered state? What can you do when you are knee deep in worries?
3. Turn a current worry into a prayer or an intention for a more desired reality.
4. Finish this statement, tune it to the state of being you desire most, and complete this sentence: ME AT _______________ Now describe how this would feel.
5. Are you open to the idea that your negative emotions are invitations to soothe a trigger and allow for personal expansion? Explain in detail.

Food SCARS-ity

Attraction Point to Ponder 5

When I see the word scarcity, my mind sees the word scar. I have so many emotional scars when it comes to growing up in a home where we had to often choose between having food in the cupboards or having gas in the car. As I think about this, I can easily recall having saltine crackers with butter on them for dinner, or even air popped popcorn, or plain pancakes. Food insecurity still exists within me as an adult and is very active, especially when a member of my family cleans out the refrigerator.

I looked up the meaning of food insecurity:

The condition assessed in the food security survey and represented in USDA food security reports—is a household-level economic and social condition of limited or uncertain access to adequate food. Hunger is an individual-level physiological condition that may result from food insecurity.

As for any definitions, we apply our own perceptions, and for this particular definition, for me, it lacks human compassion towards being in the survival mode.

In layman's terms, I was often fucking starving as a child and being a picky eater only made matters worse. Enough said.

For anyone that has ever experienced food insecurity, where you experienced a lack of consistent access to enough food, whether it was temporary or lasted a long time, the key word here is lack.

I am trusting and surrendering to the Universe to soothe any lingering feelings of lack from my childhood as I am completely triggered when someone cleans out the fridge.

Every time I witness the fridge wide open, with a garbage can below and on standby, I am triggered. I can feel my inner child wondering how the food that is being thrown out will be replaced. This feeling is frightening and activates uncertainty in me. I often leave the room. In all honesty, I tend to feel anger towards the person doing the chore. I think to myself about how wasteful that person is. There is judgment and anger. Truly, this is not how I want to live… I no longer desire to live in feelings of lack, I am ready for abundance in all aspects of my life.

Feelings of food insecurity show up not only within my thoughts but at the physical level with a tightening of the chest, and even my hands will shake. I can easily recall my hard-working mom getting paid, we would go to the grocery store, and when we returned home I would pray there would be enough food until her next paycheck. I have a distinct memory of my mom cooking for her boyfriend and being overwhelmed by the idea we even had enough to share. On one particular evening, her boyfriend asked if I knew how spaghetti was ready, not knowing, he showed me by throwing noodles at the wall to see if they would stick. I was mortified. I wanted him to leave. He was wasteful in my mind, he didn't get the big picture of my home life.

During the summer months, our local recreation center had a brown bag lunch program. I would be one of the first ones in line. I have a clear memory of seeing a mini box of raisins inside my bag. I took it home and hid it in my bedroom just in case I experienced hunger pangs while trying to sleep.

As a former educator in a high poverty school, I would receive reports of students foraging in the garbage can and I could relate. Foraging, by all means, is not a punitive act, especially for children, it is a cry for help fueled by survival instincts.

Being the primary grocery shopper in my home, I shop week to week and even day to day. I have an abundance of Tupperware and love opening a fridge full of food, no matter the state the food is in.

With feelings of lack so active in me as our fridge was recently cleaned out... I quieted my mind, and my mind went blank.

This dark moment felt frightening.

My desire is to feel better, so I monitor my breathing and tell myself that in darkness there is light. I believe there is light and allow. I ask for light and hear and see the word: KNOWING. Giving this word some thought, I realize the idea of knowing has never been a dominant part of my existence.

I sit with the word knowing and it does not feel like a match to my thoughts around food scarcity. I never experienced KNOWING when it came to food when I was growing up, *so I thought*.

Then I see a thermometer displaying a healthy body temperature of 98.6 degrees. I begin thinking about all of the times I had a fever and my body was able to recover and come back to a "normal" body temperature falling within a wide range, from 97 F to 99 F.

I then recall times where my body was freezing, and I was able to warm myself up.

Then I am presented with the memory of having an emergency c-section with my firstborn. My body fully recuperated eventually and beautifully, so much so I was able to have a second child.

I broke my leg many years ago, and to ensure recovery, I had to be non-weight bearing on my leg for many months. Eventually, I fully walked again.

Having a history of earaches, I can remember the doctor telling my mom, "Be thankful for her pain because she had a bilateral ear infection… now we can assure proper treatment and pain management."

My body not only recovers, it communicates with me. I embrace this. My trauma even communicates with me through my body, and I listen.

TRUST YOUR BODY. I hear this again, TRUST YOUR BODY.

I think about my stomach growling, and where I used to feel frightened by this, I allow it to be seen as open lines of communication between my body and me. The open lines of communication have existed so much that I am still here. I am still here.

It is at the moment I feel emotional because I haven't offered my physical body the appreciation she deserves. I am indeed still here, and my body is amazing. She is not only a survivor but also a thriver. My mind, body and soul have been a cohesive team all along.

The download I then receive is: *IT IS NOT ABOUT FOOD INSECURITY, IT IS ABOUT BODY SECURITY.*

I am still here, there was always enough and my beautiful body made damn sure I survived.

I begin to explore the idea of BODY SECURITY. I feel myself giving myself a hug. I don't remember ever even hugging her. This is an emotional moment for me as I realize, when I felt like we didn't have anything, I still had something. My powerful functioning body worked for me when there was so little to work with, and I feel so much appreciation.

I desire to now envision a member of my family cleaning out the refrigerator, and in my mind, I allow myself to volunteer to help. This would be a first for me. I am revising my story by re-visioning my story. As I allow for cognitive restructuring, I am able to reformulate old beliefs and allow new ones in. I tap into the magnificence of my physical body, I allow feelings of being secure in her power, and see myself throwing away food that was ready to be disposed of. This feels liberating. I close this meditation with a KNOWING there was always enough, and there will always be enough. I am still here, my life has always been and will continue to be, abundant.

65

1. Explore your food issues in terms of availability. Do you have food scarcity similar to my own, or do you have food abundance issues where you possibly overbuy to assure there is enough? Most importantly, do any feelings of lack exist within you when it comes to food?

2. How has your body served you in terms of recovery, offer examples. Write out statements of appreciation for your body.

3. What does BODY SECURITY mean to you, are you open to shifting from the idea of food insecurity to body security? Explain.

4. In the moments of your life where you possibly felt as if you had nothing, what are the somethings you had that kept you going? YOU ARE STILL HERE.

5. What is a revised behavior you can offer towards any feelings of lack.? Envision yourself engaging in this behavior, feel the liberation of letting go of thoughts, feelings and behaviors that no longer serve you. STEP INTO YOUR KNOWING. You can reregulate your emotions and alter or abandon targeted behavior with the power of your mind.

This Life is my Party and I will cry if I want to....

Attraction Point to Ponder 6

When I think of ourselves as infants, we cry because of hunger, there is a need for a diaper change, or maybe they don't feel good or simply there is a need to be held.

No matter what the reason...crying as a baby is an acceptable form of communication.

Something happens to the perception of tears as we get older. When I was in second grade, it was announced that my beloved elementary school was closing due to the lack of structural integrity should there be an earthquake. To make matters worse, my dad moved out unexpectedly by simply leaving a note on the kitchen table. I went from a two parent household with a stay at home mom to a single parent household with a working mom. So yes, there were tears of grief, many of them. My mom decided to take me to the doctor because she felt I was too sensitive to the big world around me and she was genuinely concerned.

I remember going to the doctor thinking he would magically stop my tears, instead, he looked at my mom and said, "Let life harden her."

What in the actual fuck?

Trust me when I say that the fear of life hardening me was unbearable throughout all of my years.

Later, as a Psychology major in college, I learned the etymology of the word hysterical. It comes from the Latin hystericus (of the womb). This is a condition exclusively associated with women where behaviors are deemed uncontrollably and neurotically insane due to the dysfunction of the uterus. We then think of the origin of hysterectomy, the actual removal of the uterus as a result. This etymology illustrates how female mental states are unpredictably characterized by emotional outbursts.

I continue to cry hysterically at times, I did as a child, and once in a while, I still do as an adult. I am not open to a hysterectomy to fix my tears, the very historical premise of this is absurd and rooted in nonsense, I am, however, open to feeling better.

This last week, I cried to a family member over the phone, and afterwards I had lingering feelings of shame because I felt shameful because I displayed weakness. Shame has always been an unwelcome emotional agent in my life. Feelings of shame show up after living with my thumb in my overwrought tears dyke for weeks and feelings of shame exist when my overflowing tear ducts finally burst. Instead of shame, feelings of appreciation should have instead dominated because when the crying pipes finally opened wide up, my relative was there to listen and I was able to unapologetically be myself.

The lingering shame from my breakdown needed to be soothed. Sometimes I feel like there are unspoken consequences for not being able to handle my inner shit, as if I have come completely unhinged.

I close my eyes and feel actual tears coming down my cheeks, I have tears for all of the times I have been told to calm down, I have tears for the value judgments placed on human emotions, I have tears behind my desires to adequately express myself without stigmatization.

I immediately see falling leaves all around me. I live to see the beauty of leaves falling off of trees in the fall, yet I still see the wonder of trees in winter, spring and summer. Trees offer oxygen and aesthetic value year around. With or without leaves, trees have value. With or without tears, we have value. The cycle of life allows for change, these are our seasons.

I then think of Ecclesiastes 3:1-8:

For everything there is a season, a time for every activity under heaven. A time to be born and a time to die. A time to plant and a time to harvest.

For every THING, there is a season. The things include tears. Tears are the things. Feel the wanted and the unwanted.

Tears represent our personal seasons of sadness, happiness, renewal and growth. Our tears are intentional and the Universe's influence on them should be acknowledged and appreciated. I can remember being a little girl and learning over and over that, yes, for everything there is a season, meaning that God, the Universe, you have various circumstances that are orchestrated behind the scenes with higher purpose and intentionality.

I am realizing that our tears are underrated. Tears are evidence that we are shifting energies. They taste salty because they were not meant to be swallowed. The saying "swallow your tears" is total bullshit. When someone tells us to do this, they are telling us to hide that we are upset, to basically control our emotions, not for our own well-being, but for others.

Tears are indeed meant to be felt and observed. Your level of apathy vs. empathy vs. sympathy may even be measured with tears. Tears are our opportunities to close gaps between empty energy where there is a lack and full energy, where there is love.

Imagine a journey from lack to love.

I begin to see my tears as confetti, as my body's celebration in my ability to feel. Tears can be joy spilling over, or they can be a release of emotions that are no longer serving you. No matter the meaning behind your tears, when you cry, you are making room for more joy if you open to better feeling thoughts.

You are your own emotional gatekeeper, you give meaning to your thoughts, emotions, and feelings.

There are no coincidences, only cooperative incidents, as Abraham Hicks describes.

We know Ecclesiastes 3:1-8: affirms two important reminders: our situations are not forever, and the things we go through in life are not in vain.

Like the seasons of a calendar year, you can be certain the current season you are in will pass. As the seasons change, circumstances will change. Allow your moments of contrast to offer purpose...breakthrough your bullshit by showing the Universe you are evolving with the changing seasons. No matter what, make peace where you are.

I strongly feel that we all can get through our dark valleys of hardship and sorrow.

The most important download I received was: *We have the power to enter new seasons when we allow for alignment after a crying session.* The end of a crying session may feel like contrast but may actually be your greatest moment for expansion. I had never thought about this before. I was being guided to note the emotions one feels after crying, and to see this is an opportunity to fill your grid with higher emotions like relief, satisfaction, love, and freedom. Enter the energy realm of trust and faith not only with the Universe but also with you, render yourself worthy.

Think about this, when we finish crying, someone may ask us if we feel better, and often we say yes. If the answer is yes, create and imagine the life you desire from this better feeling state.

Be gentle with yourself.

If after crying you feel relief, juice on this feeling for as long as possible.

If after crying you feel satisfaction, juice on this feeling for as long as possible.

If after crying you feel freedom, juice on this feeling for as long as possible.

BE IN YOUR BEING.

Welcome your negative emotion to introduce you to positive emotions. See tears with the same beauty we see falling leaves. And when they fall, be reminded that when our phone's battery is low, we charge it, when tires need air, we pump them up and when gas tanks are on empty, we fill our tanks.

The moments when tears fall are also opportunities for rebirth and revitalization.

Feel the vibrational flow towards your desires. Again, if you feel better, create better. Be in the receptive mode.

There is power in knowing our observations of our current circumstances may propel us towards our desires or have us in a holding pattern. Your perceptions of the circumstance are often the cause of so much pain, and we all have the ability to mold your perceptions to a place of preference. When we feel better, our vibrational frequencies will emit evidence of personal expansion.

Ultimately, in the discomfort we can allow for comfort.

Those people who are judging you as a cry baby are not in the same vibrational vicinity as you, don't feel or hear what they mean, feel and hear what your emotional guidance system is showing you. Have trust that our physical reality offers evidence of how well you are doing with shifting your emotions towards your real self and your desired life.

I now feel at peace knowing that crying may actually alter the electromagnetic energy waves we emit for the better. When we cry, we are changing the rate of our overall well-being and this can be felt at the cellular level and for our benefit.

Allow the unfolding. Release your own greatness that exists within.

When I now think of being done crying my heart out, I have a new appreciation for those moments where I feel lighter and more buoyant. Those moments where I can float with ease guide me. I think of the salt water taste of tears, and I continue to feel buoyant... tears self-soothe, tears promote a sense of well-being, tears help us float to the surface instead of being weighed down. Keeping afloat because of our tears; embrace the idea that tears are not sinking us, they are saving us. Everything is energy, and tears shift energy. When we cry we can feel the Heavens or the Universe wipe away our teardrops, or we can see their drops on our pillows, our clothing, or a surface. Whether they are from a place of pain or joy, tears are opportunities for reflection. When teardrops fall, the still water can offer striking depth and perception as we let go of distortions and see how perfect the moment is.

For every thing there is a season, and for every tear, there is a reason to feel better.

I close with being reminded of the Japanese Proverb: "A crying child thrives," and I add, so does a crying adult, if the individual allows themselves to do so. Crying is thriving.

1. How were tears perceived by the adults who raised you? What sayings did you hear when it came to crying?
2. What emotions do you have towards crying as an adult?
3. Are you open to the idea that tears are open to shifting energy? Explain. What desires do you have that would offer feelings of relief, freedom, satisfaction, and love? How can you bring those emotions into your current reality?
4. How do you typically feel after a good cry? Are you open to creating better in the moments where you feel better?
5. What dominant thoughts about yourself weigh you down? What feelings, thoughts, or emotions can you release, so you feel lighter? When do you feel emotionally buoyant, meaning you are floating through life with ease?

Being in WHELM

Attraction Point to Ponder 7

I have worked since I was fourteen years old, I am now fifty plus. It's been almost 4 decades straight of professional enterprise on some level. I have worked and been a student at the same time, I worked with young children, I have worked on days where I didn't sleep the night before, I worked on days where I cried driving to work, and I have worked on days when my life's ground felt like it fell out from underneath me because I was so torn between my role as a mom versus my role as an employee. With all of this, I recently decided to take a one year leave, and throughout this last year, I have felt like I should be wearing a scarlet L around my neck for Loser.

As I reflected on the possibility of taking a leave, I paid tribute to the hard-working parents of the world who do the heavy lifting of raising kids while going to work exhausted and expected to perform to high standards. We have created a village where we have normalized glorifying working hard with no regard for an individual's mental health. As a teacher, I exercised at the crack of dawn, I ate a cold lunch at my desk, I held my pee, I went to work sick because creating sub notes is cumbersome, I presented myself as bubbly when all I wanted was bubble-wrap around me protecting me from total depletion.

My friend recently shared a quote with me:

"We're expected to work like we aren't mothers and mother like we don't work."

I would go on to replace mother with the word, parent. We're expected to work like we aren't parents and parent like we don't work.

Too much has been asked of all of us, there I said it, and for one year my highest desire was to stop living in the TOO MUCH.

Coming to the tragic reality that I was even too exhausted to make peace where I am, I knew it was time to get pieces of my life back. What I did not anticipate was the reaction from others.

This need to hit the pause button was ignited as I was approaching my fiftieth birthday, how the hell was I already turning fifty? I have lived for half a century. As a senior in high school, I told my dad that one day I would be an author, and now I sometimes feel like my life has been a flash in the pan. No excuses, the bottom line is I am middle-aged and my desire to fulfill my life's sole purpose is stronger than ever. Being tuned in to my inspired impulses, I am following them, I finally feel like I am on my path. As my life path feels lit up, unfortunately, I have others who are trying to dim my light with their judgment. I am over the idea of others placing their own life's requirements on me, the emotion behind this is frustration. Frustration because where the hell were these people when my emotional empire was crumbling, attention to my psychological fall would have been welcomed. How absurd is it to be getting negative attention for moving towards my mental health? The absurdity of it all requires an energetic shift from me because I do not want to resist my alignment during this valuable time, or ever. There appears to be a disturbing dysfunction among humans, whether it is a conditioned response or not.

We tend to celebrate when someone experiences upward mobility in the work-place, but less so when someone chooses upward mobility in the headspace.

I am choosing to disallow the opinion of others, saying we should work until we retire and then have fun. This is not me determined to be right, I let all that go a long time ago, this is me being deliberate to live in alignment, meaning, TO BE WHO I REALLY AM.

As I quieted my mind, I heard *LIFE IS A HIGHWAY*, which seemed a little cliche to me. I then saw an interstate road and could see cars driving on it. I sat with this feeling of being on a road trip for a long time, it gave me the feeling of getting away from it all. A fun group or solo road trip is good for the soul. Feelings of freedom come over me.

When I think of my favorite road trips, despite the planning and the packing, I am in charge. It is typically me behind the wheel. I appreciate controlling the time of departure, possibly the arrival time, and going non-stop if I desire, or making frequent stops. I love listening to music, and I love seeing new sights. FLEXIBILITY FREEDOM is my jam.

I begin to think further on the idea of a road trip, and I apply it to my life. It is me behind the wheel, so why am I putting others behind the wheel? When I think about others staying in their own lane by minding their own business, I can tell myself to stay in my own lane as well. There is no reason I should be allowing others to steer me away from things that I find satisfying to me. My parents, my employers, and society are expecting me to do things I don't want to do…this causes resistance. My desires are bigger than other people's expectations. I have something calling me, and this is my lane.

As I continue on my mental road trip, I think about the frequent stops I make when I am driving. When I am hungry, I stop and eat. When I am tired, I stop and rest. At this moment, I thought of what fast food meant to my world, it wasn't food that was cooked fast for my convenience, it was food I ate fast because I was so damn busy. I consumed food quickly because life was consuming me. Then when I think of rest on a road trip, I think of REST AREAS and in our state of Washington, they occur about every forty miles. I have gone almost 40 years without giving my life any area of rest. Not ok, I should have pulled over a long time ago.

My soul wanted to settle in now, and enjoy the ride from a place of being satiated, satisfied and rested.

I begin to appreciate how my maps app reroutes me when there is congestion ahead, this is how I see my inner being. My inner being reroutes me to my path of least resistance and the vibration of my journey rises.

With this, I embody the idea that everyone is on their own journey.

I began to think about how much I appreciate the gift of support from others and I randomly thought of Matryoshka dolls. I have not seen one of these dolls since I was a little girl.

I googled the purpose of Matryoshka dolls, which are colorful and beautifully painted wooden nesting dolls:

Matryoshka dolls are a traditional representation of the mother carrying a child within her and can be seen as a representation of a chain of mothers carrying on the family legacy through the child in their womb. Furthermore, matryoshka dolls are used to **illustrate the unity of body, soul, mind, heart, and spirit.**

Matryoshka came from the Latin word "mater," which means "mother." Matryoshka dolls are a feminine representation of the mother carrying a child within her and carrying on the family legacy through the child in their womb.

Two things come to mind here: I think about the act of breaking the doll apart only to reveal smaller ones inside. As each figure varies in size, I realize I have decided how big or how small I want to show up in this world. My showing up is in my hands and not in the hands of others. Then I begin to think of the classical style of the Matryoshka and how it embodies the significance of a mother and her role in the family as one. I want to leave a legacy as an uplifter, not only for my children but for the entire collective. The time is now, no more laters. I have the here and now, and I am done living in the world where I will get it done tomorrow… future talk now feels like excuse-making and is very assuming.

This was a crazy meditative journey from road trips to Matryoshka dolls, but as I think of the best trips of my life, I think of souvenirs. The doll is a souvenir in my mind, a reminder of why I am on this road trip we call life.

We are here for joy but I also believe we are here to leave souvenirs behind as demonstrated in our legacy. *The divine download I appreciate is: The emotional and eternal guideposts I follow are from me for me, and not from others for them.* Be selfless, I tell myself as I close out this meditation. Selfishness is what I experience from others as they require me to be what they want, and this will keep tapping the brakes of your momentum. By choosing a year or so of being underwhelmed instead of overwhelmed I am accelerating towards my desires with diving timing. This is the ultimate souvenir I can offer myself, not only the gift of time, but knowing I am determining how big or small I show up with my inspirations as opposed to motivations. Motivation is a whelm of effort, and inspiration is a whelm of ease. I am choosing ease, and anyone who disagrees can be tuned out of my frequency, I am changing the radio station... just like I would on a road trip. They can even leave my lane. I am making peace in my never-ending journey, I am doing life for me not them.

1. If you were to go back in time, what was a life desire you created that has yet to come to fruition? Are you on an individual journey where you are going in the direction of your desires, or are there other individuals in your life's car putting on the brakes of your dreams? What are your roadblocks and what is your higher self's path of least resistance?

2. Explore how others coming into your lane may be holding you back from following your soul's life purpose. How can you allow the judgment of others to serve you? Explore how you can stay in your lane by allowing your personal alignment to be a priority.

3. Are you allowing others to determine how much you show up in this world? Explain. Do you have a desire to stop playing small and show up in a big way, knowing you are the creator of your reality?

4. What is the souvenir in terms of legacy that you want others to remember you by? What can you do to enhance your legacy now?

5. When we think of motivation, we think of effort and being goal-oriented. What inspires you, what path lights you up? How can you allow more ease into your life? Think of inspirations not motivations.

When a Botched Recipe Makes Life Yummy

Attraction Point to Ponder 8

One intention I have for my life is to get squeaky clean with my vibration because I have some amazing desires that I would love to come to fruition. As I explored my limiting beliefs, already knowing if I think I have limitations, this is a limitation, I realized I have a *fear of being seen* renting space for free within my subconscious.

In middle school, I was the frontrunner for the SPELLING BEE. The event was an all school event where everyone was invited to watch, similar to an assembly. One feather in my cap was my stellar spelling skills. I was born ready, so I thought. The hosting teacher announced it was my turn by announcing my name, and the audience roared, I felt the adrenaline at the molecular level. She said, "Recipe... My grandmother recently baked my favorite cookie recipe... recipe." I smiled with confidence as I stood on the stage in front of the entire student body. I looked out into the audience and said rapidly into the microphone, "R.E.C.E.PE." The teacher looked at me and said, "I apologize, that is incorrect." I was mortified, the adrenaline, the overconfidence and my speedy response caused me to be careless, and you could hear a pin drop. I sat down, and what I didn't realize was how the events that would follow would impact me. Although my fellow students were compassionate, I still was given the new nickname, RECIPE. Fuck my life, I remember thinking these words like it was yesterday. I told myself, I would never go on a stage again.

Looking back, I felt like I blinked the day of the SPELLING BEE, and I would later try to train myself to never blink again. I now remind myself constantly of the power of the pause. One small moment felt like my life had changed forever. Not blinking and pausing meant living deliberately by being a high self-monitor. From that point forward, I micromanaged my behaviors to the point of exhaustion to avoid any form of public embarrassment.

Realistically, there is only so much high self-monitoring one can do, and I believe the Universe has a fun sense of humor, so trust me when I say I have other embarrassing slips in behavior.

Now with aging, changes in my physical appearance, and well, life happening, I can feel a stronger fear of being seen, at a time when I am ready to entirely show up as my authentic self. Fear is the dominant emotion here, along with self-doubt.

As I quieted my mind, I immediately saw a nautical telescope, a long brass monocular that I immediately looked through. Without any apprehension, I look through it to see myself way out at sea struggling, there wasn't a feeling of drowning, but a feeling of, I AM TREADING WATER and going nowhere fast. I was so far away from any shoreline. My initial instinct was to magnify the image of me and bring it in closer in order to feel like I was close to land, this did not help at all, it only made the image more real. The struggle just became more real as it was enhanced. I recently learned that when manifesting, I can ask the Universe for clarity, so that is exactly what I did. A response was offered to me with the visual of a boat's life preserver ring being tossed to me from the Universe, I grabbed on without any hesitation. So much appreciation because I know the Universe always provides. I calm down with my body, but still feel very vulnerable physically, emotionally and mentally. I then ask for further clarity. A white boat shows up, a ladder on the side, I climb up, I ascend. There is a flat white spot on the front of the boat waiting for me, I lay out on it, this feels safe, this feels like rest, I feel myself willing to let go of the struggle, I am coding for higher everything through stillness. I bask. The boat's slight movement rocks me like a baby, I allow the feeling of being in a cradle to soothe me. There I rest, there I rock, there I make the choice to detach from my fears and attach to ease. I am reminded of my energetic blueprint, what I am here for, all of what lights me up. I am willing to let the feelings of lack behind my self-sabotaging stories go. I am realigning. This all feels like a hug from the Universe, this is where my version 2.0 desires to be. The state of receiving is felt as warm tingles throughout my body. I am reminded that in peace and I receive all of it. Doing nothing is doing something. I keep allowing ease in, at this moment, I juice every ounce of nutrients as this moment in time is nourishing my soul.

As I look up to take it all in, I realize I am being brought to shore, this feels like the path of least resistance, I embrace this from a total place of alignment. There is a state of nothingness that travels through me from head to toe that offers a feeling of being completely grounded. Orgasmically present, I am shoring up my life, if you will. I am shoring up for my dreams to be seen, and from this place, I set intentions for when we dock. I expect unconditional love and feelings of freedom. I decide. I choose. It is done, and so it is.

As I got closer, I realized there were people waiting for me. This was my soul tribe, I felt a love fest greeting. I am reminded that one's vibe attracts their tribe. The boat is docked without any apprehension. As I walk ashore, I hear, "We have been waiting for you to show up!" The voices sounded so excited, the word WELCOME written using rocks. None of these people are ones that I have met before. One went on to say in the most relieving tone, "It is your message, your impact, your presence, that we desire!" These are my people, I felt it. Having only just met them, I still feel so much love for them and from them. We dance, we sing, we laugh, we allow freedom in.

I suddenly have a moment where I am reliving my old story, I hear myself asking, "Where are all of my critics?" The response from my inner being, "You exiled them to an island where they are a vibrational match for others, you are no longer a match for judgment because you are attaching higher meaning to your life's experiences." This was my journey and I embraced it.

Breathing in the idea that my old story was that I was choosing to stay out at sea, keeping me from people who were ready for me. This is a disservice to me and others. I am choosing to live my truth. Breathing out the idea that all I had to do was show up, give up struggle, allow ease in, and go to the shore with the intention to be surrounded by unconditional love and freedom. I am reminded that I have the power to mentally exile emotions, thoughts, and people that no longer serve me, any attachment to them is an illusion. I have the ability to remove negative energy from power, to dethrone it all, where judgmental people are stepping down from my life in favor of me. The exile ultimately means not giving space to my critics, and in return, I create space for my true followers, those that are ready for me. This is a level of consciousness that feels so liberating. I LOVE FREEDOM, I LOVE FREE MOVEMENT, I LOVE FREE FLOW, and I LOVE FREE-SPIRITED PEOPLE. I would rather be dancing than treading water. The life I desire of being seen has always existed, I just had to be ready to come to shore, and my followers were always there waiting for me with open arms. In a parallel Universe, this beautiful reality has always existed, and I am docked and anchored to a reality that lights me up. I am reminded of the knowledge that I am the lighthouse allowing my desires to experience a safe journey home. I allow for a moment of appreciation because I trusted the timing of this energetic shift, total thrill bumps. This life is your LOVE BOAT, you are a lighthouse, and this is your time to not only shine but to come to shore.

1. What past event(s) may be preventing you from truly showing up in your life? What specifically about this event has possibly played a role in your fear of being seen? Is it a memory, a stream of thoughts, a person, or people, or ALL OF THE ABOVE?

2. Think of the meaning of the word *EXILE*, disempower any of the above by choosing to dethrone them, take back your power, and banish them from your mental island. What memory is no longer allowed from a place of fear, and allow it to become your faith in being seen. You are an exclusive island, share how this experience has actually empowered you.

3. What feels like a *life preserver* from the Universe to you, what experience in your physical reality would offer you a feeling of ease, and what makes you feel like you are effortlessly floating towards your desires? What message or mission do you have to offer to your soul tribe? This can include family members, close friends, and followers.

4. What lights you up? We are our own lighthouses, again, what lights you up? This is a checkpoint to make sure there are no attachments to anything that is dimming your light, underneath the crap, your light is still lit, this is the time to peel back the layers so you can shine.

5. When was the last time you danced? For dance, I mean any movement that gets you out of your mental body and emotional body by moving your body. What can you do on a daily basis to allow energetic shifts throughout your entire body and tap into feelings of freedom?

For Heaven's Sake

Attraction Point to Ponder 9

I have so much guilt because I learned about my best friend's death after she had been on life support for an accidental drug overdose. I should have been by her side as she transitioned. The guilt has haunted me for several years, and the sadness around her and me not growing old together is heartbreaking. There are days I feel paralyzed by grief. Today I am going to "go there", "there" is a place with so much apprehension because I could never imagine answers that would actually make me feel better.

Since she has died, I have not wanted her in Heaven. Call me selfish, but Heaven was when she was physically here with me. I miss laughing with her, crying with her, dancing with her... I miss her being a phone call away.

As I silenced my soul, I realized IMMEDIATELY I see myself as one big teardrop, it's heavy, but it makes sense. When it comes to her, I feel like crying all of the time. Immediately, I want to feel better, and the imagery goes from being a big teardrop to a small and inviting peephole shaped as a keylock on a door, without any hesitation I look in. I see her lying in her hospital bed. This was my chance to go lay with her, go be by her side and beg her not to go, and let her feel my presence. I see myself lying next to her and pleading, please don't fucking leave me. Please fucking stay. Yet I feel myself peeking in still, like my thoughts got way ahead of me. I know I should have been there with her. I then hear her voice say to me, loud and clear, "You were there." I responded, "I should have been there physically, I am so sorry, why didn't anyone call me? I would have been there." I hear her say, "You were there." I say, "No, I wasn't, I am so fucking sorry." Tears rolling down my human cheek. Again she says, "You were there, in my last moments in my human experience, I lived out the moments where I experienced the most unconditional love, and thank you, our laughs together kept me alive for a little longer, I was given more time before I left. When we laugh together, we are always breathing life into the people around us and through us."

"I didn't get to say goodbye, and I am so sorry." I hear her say, "Why would you say goodbye? I am still here with you, there is no need to say goodbye. This peephole you see me through is to keep you at bay and not let you near me physically but to program you to feel me. When you peep through it, remember moments of unconditional love with me, look again, and only moments of joy should be seen. You can honor me by not remembering the pain I was in, but in the joy I was in."

Taking many deep breaths, I peeked again and saw us laughing at a high school football game below Seattle's Space Needle. I peeked again, and saw her and me dancing in her bedroom. It felt so safe to peek through and feel so much appreciation for our time together.

It was at this moment, I knew her passing meant an end to the physical pain she was in with her addictions but keeping her alive meant pivoting away from painful memories to ones where she was happy.

She then shared how she is with souls that she thought caused her pain while here, but now when she sees them, there are only feelings of unconditional love being exchanged, and all of them have the ability to offer that exchange with those still having a human experience.

My analytical brain wanted to know how, and she said in so many words, the essence of those who have passed are all around at all times, again, why we don't have to say goodbye, they are still here. Talk to us, feel us, think of us in our joy. Then this incredible download came hearing her voice:

Live in the essence of who we were, but also who YOU WERE when we were in physical reality.

Keep us alive with memories where we are experiencing joy, keep hospital moments at a distance, keep memories of us in pain at bay, keep memories of any arguments at bay, bring us to life by bringing in memories of when your loved ones were experiencing joy. She said loud and clear, "When you bring in memories of loved ones who left physical reality, and you sit with memories, you are honoring our legacy, but you are to also feel better, and feeling better is bringing more joy into your life, and that is what we want, more joy for all of you, not grief or guilt or sadness, more joy, feel the essence of me all around you, talk to me, and honor me through the joyful memories, joyful memories of passed loved ones will change your human experience."

BUT WHY DID YOU HAVE TO FUCKING DIE? She said, I chose to, and again you are placing emphasis on my human body, and not my soul. I left my vessel, but I am still here, feel me, talk to me, and honor me through joyful memories.

I realized I was putting so much emphasis on her pain and my guilt for not doing more. I peeped again, and I remembered joyfully driving in her grandpa's truck, and I felt she was with him now. I peeped again, and I joyfully remembered us giggling in the hallways of our high school.

I was bringing her back to life with JOY, I felt the essence of her, and I started talking aloud and crying. I have missed talking to her so much. I felt like we had so much to catch up on, and she giggled, "No, we don't, I have always been with you, if talking makes you feel better then talk, always do whatever you think will make you feel better from a place of unconditional love and know that I already feel better, I chose to die." I internalized the idea that she chose to leave her physical body, but she has never really left me. "Why am I crying, I ask her?" "Why am I sobbing so fucking hysterically at this very moment?" You are crying like someone who is having a reunion with a loved one at the airport after a long absence, we are reuniting THROUGH JOY and those are happy tears, I have been here but through feelings of guilt and grief, you are now experiencing JOY by honoring my life through memories where I had physical wellness and JOY." A reunion is not necessary because I have always been here, but in this moment, you invited different emotions, so the experience feels different.

Similar to loved ones at the airport, only this time, we are not in the DEPARTURES frequency anymore, we are in ARRIVALS. We are together after a long flight where there was turbulence due to sadness, and now we are so happy to see each other, you can really feel me. At this moment, I felt so much better. I had always heard that JOY IS THE KEY, but this saying now took on a whole new meaning. I can peek through my keyhole opening at any time and see her in joy, and this, in return, honors her in a state of physical wellness, this gives me feelings of joy, and she and I have a beautiful exchange of unconditional love.

She is no longer in physical pain, she is happy... I am choosing to no longer live in physical pain of her passing, I am choosing JOY for the both of us, this flight is on time, and I am appreciating the divine timing. I feel myself desperately wanting this moment to ever end, the clarity of her voice to stay with me in my ears, her articulate words streaming through me, and then I remembered she isn't going anywhere, she is with me *always*. I deeply breathe this thought in: if my best friend was able to allow JOY in while dying, you can allow JOY in while living. None of us are flying solo, ever, trust me. There is no need to feel alone in your journey, we are, in essence, never entirely alone. It is our time to SOAR.

· · ·

Judy Garland once said, "I have never looked through a keyhole without someone looking back." But when it comes to death, look through life's keyhole, knowing the person looking back at you is in joy, and allow that moment to give you joy. Emotional turbulence is delaying you from joy. Raising your frequency to feelings of unconditional love *and* joy is heaven here on earth where we experience smoother flights and smoother landings. Recline. Rest. Enjoy the flight.

1. If you have lost someone because the person transitioned, tap into a memory where their human self is in a state of physical wellness, peek through the keyhole, what memory gives you a vision of them in joy? Peek through two more times, what are two more memories you have where the person is in a state of physical wellness and joy?

2. Now feel the joy from them move to you and through you. Feel better, your loved ones want to see you in JOY, a mirrored emotion of how they want to be remembered. What feels different in your body by allowing JOY in?

3. Do you talk to your loved ones who have passed? If so, what responses do you hear from them from a place of unconditional love? If not, try it, and feel the essence of them listening and responding to you.

4. If you have been living in the energy of someone's DEPARTURE because of their transitioning, what would feel like the energy of ARRIVAL by allowing yourself to still feel their presence in your life through higher emotions, how might you communicate with them differently, how would you want them to see you?

5. What can you do to soothe your emotional turbulence around grief, how would your higher self desire you to grieve?

MaMartyrdom

Attraction Point to Ponder 10

My daughter recently shared with me that she was watching a movie with her friend and they turned it off because it was about divorce. I could see the impact of *everything divorce* on her face and I could feel the battering on both of us in my soul.

This moment was a big invitation towards something to calibrate on.

It has well been over a decade since my divorce, and I still grapple with the idea that I should have stayed married for the sake of my children, despite my own unhappiness. Here my beautiful seventeen old daughter, who hasn't seen her parents together since she was in kindergarten, was still showing signs of heartache. In these moments, my emotional default setting is to either go completely dead inside or feel guilt and shame. When she was very young, I asked myself if I should stay in a broken marriage where I am so broken, or break away and begin to pick up the pieces.

As I allowed my mind to be flooded with the emotions of guilt and shame, while seeing her face and the pain, as well as feeling mine, I thought about my divorce. Immediately, I see the image of a big 8 ball coming at me with the sound effect of the pool stick hitting the ball. I felt invaded. Needing to feel better, I set the 8 ball down on a pool table, but this pool table looked like one you would find in an unkept dive bar, the overall feeling felt dirty. I felt dirty. I have a strong affinity for dive bars so it wasn't the setting I desired to change, it was the 8 ball. I thought about this imagery and thought about its meaning. I have maybe played pool three times in my life, nor have I picked up one of those 8 ball fortune tellers since I was little, so why would I get this? Then it hit me like a pool stick hitting a pool ball, with an 8 ball, if a player knocks the 8 ball off the table, the player loses the game, or if the player pockets the 8 ball and commits a foul, the player loses the game. It overwhelmed me to think of all of the potential for fouls within the game of pool and I realized, within my marriage, I lived surrounded by similar pockets that gave me thoughts of being a loser. One wrong move, or if I called a shot wrong, I lose or I am forfeited from the life of happiness I desire. Within my marriage, the perspective I chose to practice absolute feelings of low self-worth from the kitchen to the bedroom, nothing felt like a game room where there was fun to be had.

My focus became on the ball, and my imagination changed it into a skee-ball, and I immediately had a memory of taking my children to a family arcade on multiple road trips as a single mom, we would have the best time ever. They would get their wiggles out, we would spend freely and play and play and play. I began to feel better.

I then zoom in and see a tall version of me standing there in front of a skeeball machine, holding a wooden ball, and the imagery had me in heels and trust me, I never wear heels. I stand there wobbly, not very well balanced, yet balanced, empowered by being the one who actually holds the ball. This is a beautiful image of me post-divorce. I stand there in dise-quilibrium, but I hold the ball, owning my life's instability. I look fun, I look silly, I look free. This is the image my children have had of me in my post-divorce years…the majority of their upbringing.

Within my marriage, I did feel like a loser, and I played as if I was going to lose, lose meaning make a mistake at any given moment. A version of me holding a pool stick with an 8 ball on the table is one who is unsure, worried and apprehensive. My children would have had front row seats to a mom who played small and didn't show up entirely for her life out of fear of making a mistake. I can't help but imagine for a moment how different my grown children would have turned out as a result, but I refuse to live in the world of WHAT-IFS, so I move on.

I then think of myself wearing heels while playing skeeball, and despite my potential to fall down, I know I modeled a mom who would get back up. The influence of me maybe didn't feel entirely on stable ground. Yet I held the ball of my destiny, and they experienced the beautiful ripple effect of my sticktoitiveness and my ability, for the most part, to stand solo and tall when faced with adversity.

Making the conscious choice to hold the ball is how I regained a sense of self and changed the trajectory of what kind of parent I was. This gave me head to toe feelings of peace. The person I was within my marriage was not the mom I wanted to be for my children. The person I am now, because I showed courage to leave the pool table, is who I loved modeling to both of them. Has it at times felt unstable, like standing on shaky ground? Absolutely. Do my grown children have memories of a mom who got back up every time she fell down? Most certainly. Would I risk fouling with an 8 ball and live miserably in a marriage for my children? No, and that no is without any regrets. Do I love holding my own power and feeling so much happiness within my own free will? TOTALLY. Most importantly, was I the best version of myself from a place of free will for the three of us? Damn straight.

As I am writing this, I realize there will be people saying OK, but was divorce necessary to experience free will and empowerment? In terms of my own life, I offer an unapologetic YES!!! I LOVE THE SINGLE MOM I WAS WHILE RAISING MY KIDS, and they reaped the benefits of her daily, that is my final answer, and I am sticking to it. Empowerment.

After my meditation, I went to my daughter and told her that I was a better version of being her mom because I was divorced. I wanted to apologize but I stopped myself.

I am not sorry for choosing personal empowerment over marital devourment because of my own limitations.

She said, "I know, and I love you." She knows, she has known all along our story, and thoughts of divorce making her sad are welcomed, she is healing, and this is her personal journey. She knows that I believed in my core that good parenting means showing up as my authentic self, she would have never wanted me to fake it while we made it…to her high school graduation.

Then thinking of my son, I am reminded of this powerful moment when he openly proclaimed, "I do not come from a broken family, I come from a fixed one." Perspective is everything.

After my daughter and I talked, I walked down the hall and thought of selective sayings about taking shots in life. I have heard along the way, "There is always a shot, you just have to find it." None of us are stuck. I think of my incredible will, and know that for any of us, it's the will for a better life that makes for a better team player. I live with total confidence the three of us make a great team, and that is all that matters. I now go back to another road trip memory where EMINEM is blaring and the three of us are singing the song, "Lose Yourself", and I feel the lyrics, "Look, if you had one shot or one opportunity to seize everything you ever wanted in one moment would you capture it, or just let it slip." Singing the words aloud, I smile and reflect, knowing I captured it all. With this, I am at peace.

1. Where in your life do you have the feeling of potentially fouling at any given moment? Look around, do you see pockets where there are rules that make you feel like a loser? Make these thoughts irrelevant by focusing on the pockets of your success.
2. Knowing that you hold the ball of destiny in your hands with your thoughts, feelings and emotions, what inspired impulse could you follow today to live a more empowering life?
3. Are you unapologetically you? If not, where are you making excuses about your life to please others and what they think your life should be? If yes, explain and include how you might enhance this feeling further.
4. Are you able to find stability in your instability? By that, how are you maintaining balance in your life?
5. Tune in, whether you are a parent or not, tap into a memory where you are having a total blast. What are you doing, what are you feeling, and what are your surroundings like? How can you bring this version of yourself into your current reality more often?

Money Does Indeed Grow On Trees

Attraction Point to Ponder 11

So many desire to manifest money, but I know people often have abundance blocks and limiting beliefs around finances. I have a core belief that if you can unlock your blocks, seeing blocks simply as padlocks, then you can attract more. Although actual dollars are what many think they want, in actuality, what most really want is a feeling of abundance, security or freedom that comes with having it. After so much inner work, I know the following about me:

I live very aware of whether I am activating feelings of lack or abundance.

For me, lack brings feelings of scarcity, and abundance brings feelings of overflow.

Growing up, my single mom made minimum wage after my parents divorced. We had countless moments where feelings of scarcity were dominant. We did not have an entertainment budget, had very few frivolous spending moments, couponing was necessary, and so much penny pinching to make ends meet.

I started babysitting as young as I can remember, at age fourteen I worked in fast food to help with the essentials. In college, I had three summer jobs and held two work study jobs just to get through. As for adulting, working for a non-profit organization and being an educator never felt abundant as well. I even managed to marry someone admirably frugal.

With all that I have endured and for what has been imprinted upon me when it comes to money, I remain committed to reframing my engrained false financial beliefs. I can recall learning about a psychological study that claimed poor children are more likely to feel financially powerless as adults than children from middle-income homes. Living aware of these findings, I have devoted myself to staying in the energy of abundance by embodying my power as a creator. I am able to tap into abundance through feelings of freedom, satisfaction and relief. Somedays, like today, however, my monetary fears still manage to creep in and rear their ugly head.

On this particular morning, the question, "Where is the money going to come from?" completely took over my being. As I silenced my mind after getting this topic cooking in my thoughts, this question was playing itself out on a loop in my mind over and over and over. In my head, I was puzzled because I thought I had done so much clearing work around the topic of finances, I had already had a huge epiphany with "The money always showed up, there was always enough." This was a huge break-through for me, so where are my fears coming from?

As I quieted my mind, the image representing my fears immediately surfaced as a RED MAPLE LEAF. My grandparents lived near the Canadian border. As I pictured the Canadian flag with the single maple leaf on it, I was thinking the leaf had something to do with my grandma and grandpa who married after meeting during World War 2. Talks of depression, food rations, and hearing them say, "Waste not, want not," were recalled. Memories of conversations I heard around money kept coming in, and the more they came in, the flatter the leaf became, the redder it became, the more still it became, lifeless yet with color so red it was unbearable to the human eye. Changing the color of it to green felt better, and allowing myself to see an alive and thriving tree felt even better. The money phrases I heard growing up kept gushing in now concerning when I would ask for any type of allowance, "What do you think, money grows on trees?" and "Do you think I am made of money?" These two questions alone imply that money does not come easily, a person has to work hard for it, and it is possibly a limited resource, so be careful how you spend it. These verbal memories made me cringe. Within my mental money tree were branches of shame and guilt. I could see a version of me, a child under the tree with her head on her knees, crying. The shame and guilt for having material desires were there, and the tears were real.

I felt the tree calling me to get up, to stand alongside the tree. I not only stood up, I hugged the tree feeling the energy. My bare feet began to experience a grounding sensation like I had never felt before. I could feel the strength of the tree as it stood supported by its roots, and I could feel the strength increase in me as I rooted myself into our planet earth. As I allowed this sensation to travel from my feet to my head, I began to understand what a true energy exchange is, and basked in the appreciation for the abundance I was feeling. In this heightened state, I chose to go back in time, with this feeling of abundance within me, and be with my grandparents. Ironically, it was so easy for me to see my grandparents' conversations as generational, so no harm, no foul. After basking for a while in a delicious and abundant memory of eating homemade jam and scones with my grandparents, I became more aware of where my wonky energy around money existed. The single moms I was surrounded by while growing up modeled lack, no fault of their own. My childhood neighborhood was packed full of divorced women working minimum wage jobs and I was influenced by the upbringings of other latchkey children. As a little girl I heard the moms often say aloud, "What do you think there is a money tree in the backyard?" There are also other phrases like, "Do you think I have money to burn?" jam packed in my mind with shame and guilt still very active for me as the witness and the receiver.

Taking many deep breaths, I allow for the shift of energy to move away from lack towards abundance, my body immediately feels different, less tense.

I first feel freedom, satisfaction and relief in my body and I am able to transpose my being to a memory of vacationing in Hawaii. Feeling the hot sand beneath me, experiencing the freshness of the hotel's sheets, and the dining out moments amped up my abundant state. Now I allow myself to explore the idea of money growing on trees from a higher perspective. Whether or not money is made of wood pulp, cotton fibers, or linen... everything is energy, and energy can neither be created nor destroyed. I felt the energy exchange from this grounding experience, and realized the answer was a resounding YES! EVERYTHING IS ENERGY! This felt affirming and liberating.

Peace came over me because in this moment I am reassured that I do not have to perpetuate the lack perspectives the adults around me chose to practice. I AM ABUNDANCE, money flows to me and through me, I get paid to be me, money is an energy exchange because when I spend money I expect to get it back. Not only has there always been enough, money comes to me effortlessly and through multiple means. This is my story.

I now vision my tree again and all of the emotions I associate with abundance and these are my dominant branches: love, satisfaction, ease, freedom, relief, and excitement. No more fear, just trust.

As I allow myself to feel the seismic shifts in my body, I vividly see an imaginary mom shadow writing a note to a school's nurse's office, I could see the flow of her pen. She was present as if this moment was really happening. The note read, "Please excuse Elizabeth from attachments to her past that no longer serve her, she is allowing herself to detach from a cycle of generational poverty modeled to her as a child." The perspective I was practicing was based on adult statements I had internalized, and their words may have been influenced by their parents and so and so on. I felt the paper of the note to the nurse as it was handed to me, paper, just like money, does grow on trees, everything is energy. This imaginary kinesthetic moment was so affirming on many levels, even my money memories felt different to me now. I smile. I am uplifted yet I need to rest. Vividly in my mind, I now see the treehouse built in my backyard's tree by my dad before he moved out. I crawl in it and lay down, and I thank our planet, and all of the trees and all of our earth's beauty, and my family, for offering me a life of abundance. All of them have provided for me on some level.

No matter what I have been through, no matter what I have heard, there was always enough, and now I know there was even more than enough. Again, everything is energy. I am still here. I have a 100% track record for getting through my worst financial days as I root myself in feelings of total appreciation. Money is not the root of all evil, it is grounded in the root of a perspective you are choosing to practice. I breathe these words in, and the air feels fresh, and I feel the oxygen from the trees in my soul. I close this meditation with feelings of knowing that the money will show up, it always has and it always will.

1. What are the phrases you heard growing up around money?
2. From a place of seeing money as energy, how can you offer a leveled up perspective on the experiences you have had, and the sayings you heard? Feel your perspective change at the visceral level, feel your new perspective.
3. What is a higher emotion branch you can add to your tree? Explain. Are you open to the idea that spending money can be an energy exchange…you can spend knowing the money will come back to you, explore this.
4. We know that freedom is the frequency of abundance, what gives you feelings of freedom?
5. Set a financial intention from your new perspective around money:

I choose:

I expect:

I desire:

Ghostingbusters

Attraction Point to Ponder 12

I recently heard the quote, "Maybe you were meant to meet, but that does not mean you were meant to be." I found myself feeling overwhelming guilt towards those in my life I have not stayed in touch with. It makes me so sad that I have ghosted people from my past. I feel so at fault for not being meant to be part of this quote. Guilt, guilt poured over me, the feeling was almost too much.

Looking back, I believe I often abandoned people before they abandoned me.

I think I did it to them because I assumed they would do it to me eventually.

If my own dad could abandon me at age 9, anyone can.

My visualization began with a rusty red and orange dumpster, this was very unexpected but very real. Immediately, I knew the feeling tone I had created within my relationships with so many had felt like a large fucking dumpster fire, a toxic wasteland with shit fumes rising from the top. It all felt like garbage. Immediately I stop the fumes, as I strongly desire to see and feel different.

And who would make an immediate and unexpected cameo in my thoughts, none other but OSCAR THE GROUCH. I felt surprise and relief come over my body, I have not thought about Oscar for decades. Here I am at age 50, with grown children, and Sesame Street imagery appears. Why? I ask my inner being, WHY? I wait. I hear different Oscar quotes in my mind, "If you think about it, a great big pile of trash is pretty," and, "There will be more trash tomorrow," and of course, "I love trash!" I smile to myself, I hear these sayings differently now as an adult, there is a new meaning to them. Then I see Oscar surrounded by friends even though he lives in a garbage can, friends who genuinely love him. I enjoy this moment because I loved watching Sesame Street; I grew up making friends with the best characters of all, Snuffaluffagus, Big Bird, Ernie and Bert, and so many more. I always felt so much unconditional love while watching all of them. I see all of the wonderful characters standing there, not a care in the world that their friend Oscar lives in a garbage can. I feel the love they have for one another, and even for me. I am able to tap into this feeling effortlessly. This was powerful imagery, but not the message, I felt more coming. I then see a 3 X3 grid, putting all of my favorite characters into nine rectangular boxes, myself in the center box, head down and sad. I am hearing the song, "One of these things (is not like the others), One of these things is not like the others, One of these things doesn't belong." The song then asks, "Can you tell which thing is not like the others? I then see myself upset, I have always felt like not one of the others, as if I DON'T BELONG. Always. I feel the finger-pointing. I have felt targeted. I feel shame, so much shame. Feeling as if EVERYONE IN THE WORLD watching the show guessed it was ME that does not belong, and they were absolutely right. I want to hide and cry and disappear from my square, asking why my inner being would give me this imagery.

Then in the most loving singing voices, I hear, "You are not like the others and it is OK, it is OK." IT IS OK TO NOT BE LIKE THE OTHERS! Say it loud so the people in the back can hear it, IT IS OK NOT TO BE LIKE THE OTHERS! I felt like I had waited my whole life to hear these words. I tell myself, "I am OK to not be like the others, it is OK." I breathe these words in, I pause, I breathe them out, creating space for more of this message. I FEEL THESE WORDS. I feel the release of tears. I say to them again, IT IS OK, I am choosing to be done conditioning my body to a state of fear of not fitting in, giving so much power to the sequence of events that happened during my perceived trauma. I have been living in utter fear that if I keep people in my life too long, they will see my garbage, so I need to throw them away first before they throw me away. As a result, I have treated people like yesterday's newspaper, ultimately making them old news before I become just that. This does not have to be my truth. This does not have to be my story, my front page headline can read differently. I suddenly have a very big desire to be ME standing in my own garbage can, knowing I can still be surrounded by unconditional love. This feels powerful and liberating. I see the image of me climbing out of my rectangle within the grid, all of my Sesame Street friends clapping in support. Then this download comes in loud and clear, *"Step out of the comfort of your self-created box, and allow the discomfort to serve you towards your desires."* Maybe because I am surrounded by the most unconditional love from all of the most well-known characters on Sesame Street, I step out of my rectangle with ease, it feels safe, I thank them all and appreciate the divine timing because I feel my readiness.

Then another very powerful download occurs, *"Stepping out of your SAFETY NET allows one to cast a wider net towards all of their desires and dreams."* The small space of my safety net keeps me playing small. It's comfortable, but it is the discomfort of deciding to show up, where I can encapsulate the life I am here to live. I milk this moment. I bask. Feelings of freedom are fusing themselves together, there is a rewiring taking place as I am reminded how I think and how I feel plays a role in my destiny.

I then began to harmonize the Sesame Street theme song in my mind, "Sunny day sweepin' the clouds away…" With my conscious mind, I know I want to be healthy and free of my analytical mind, and it felt so good to slow my thoughts down with the Sesame Street song I grew up with. I was allowing joy and inspiration in, and I then tweaked the lyrics a bit, "Sunny **thoughts** taking my clouds away.." I am ready to fire and wire on different circuits, my story goes from being hardwired with uneasiness by who I am to being OK with feeling different from all others. This is an empowering circuit flow. I am rewiring to allow the power of stepping out of my comfort zone. There is a grounding surge happening where I know I can respond to the thoughts that cause me discomfort by changing my internal weather pattern and circuit board. I have the power to take my clouds away and all of the negative charges. I am a powerful creator. Where Sesame Street was my teacher for so many different reasons, I embody the idea that *I am the teacher to my thoughts.*

My quantum reality comes from thoughts that are loving and creating. It is my higher thoughts, emotions and actions that create the life I desire. I am the teacher, I create the lesson plans for myself from a state of higher consciousness while paying homage to all of my teachers along the way. I am being defined by the visions of my future... my *personality is my personal reality*, the time is now to level up and create from my quantum self, I am a spiritual being having a human experience. It is OK to be me. In fact, it is more than OK. I am breaking patterns of predictable comfort and stepping out of my rectangular safe haven to a place where my body is no longer my mind, where my passion frees me of the guilt of my past, where I *allow* people to point at me because I AM DIFFERENT. SUNNY THOUGHTS keeping the CLOUDS AWAY, this is pivoting at its finest.

Just because we have a negative thought, it does not mean it's true, all of us can reach for better feeling thoughts at any given moment. Our emotional garbage is not a dumpster fire, it's what gives us the fire in our belly, it's where our passions are created. Again, as Oscar proclaims, trash is beautiful, the trash being all of what we have endured and are. Our lives should be on Sesame Street where we are attracting others that *Come and Play, Everything's A-OK, friendly neighbors there, that's where we meet...* We get to Sesame Street by standing tall in our garbage, seeing our beauty no matter what, and surrounding ourselves and expecting unconditional love from those that are by our side no matter how we look, feel, speak, or even smell.

We are here to break weather patterns, we are here for the dumpster fire, knowing it is burning fuel for our desires, we are here to pivot if only to feel better for a few moments... we always have the power to reach for higher states of being.

I close this meditation thinking about one of my favorite quotes, "You never change your life until you step out of your comfort zone; change begins at the end of your comfort zone." *-Roy T. Bennett*

1. Are you open to the idea of living with the freedom of not necessarily having to throw away one's emotional trash, but allowing it to burn with beautiful flames by reflecting on how you can show up differently from a place of empowerment?

2. If you keep throwing people in your life away by ghosting them, is this out of fear? If so, dive deep here, where is the fear coming from? Abandonment issues? Consider that any abandonment you have experienced had nothing to do with you, how can you make another person's actions irrelevant? What if abandonment doesn't have to show up as fear but indeed an opportunity for strength because you are breaking cycles?

3. What is your personal weather pattern, for example, sunny with a chance of clouds? What would be your ideal forecast for your life?

4. If your personal forecast is gloomy, what daily habit can you bring in to help you weather the storms of your life?

5. Think of a thought about yourself that makes you feel like garbage. How can you allow your perceived emotional trash to be recycled into a valuable resource for you? Do you have people who stand by you in your emotional garbage? If so, what does unconditional love mean to you?

I Call Bull on Body Image

The topic of body image for me is heavy, this pun is intended. I have felt the struggle my entire life with people's perceptions of what I look like, what I should look like, why don't I look like what I once looked like, I could go on and on. For me, the thoughts of how I see myself take me down a long and dark alley. I know I have allowed this to be my truth for too long.

I don't even need a moment to trigger me. I live activated my self-diagnosed body dysmorphia which is my intrusive preoccupation with body defects caused by fluctuating body weight.

I am a total city girl, grew up in Seattle, my comfort zone is truly urban jungles where everything concrete and city lights is where I am home. Needless to say, as I tuned in, I saw a raging bull with horns and a nose ring. This seemed overwhelming, very invasive and foreign to me, just like being in the country feels to me. To ease my fear at this moment, I was able to tap into one memory where my sister and I took a walk in the country near my grandma's house, located in the backwoods, and we actually saw a bull and the bull came fiercely running towards us and we ran like hell. Thankfully the bull was at a distance and in fenced quarters, so yes, we got away. Of course, there was also the mechanical bull stage in my early 20s, but I chose sitting at the bar vs. sitting on the bull. Riding a mechanical bull was a hard pass for me.

Allowing my memory to wander a bit did not fix the fact that my subconscious was shoving an aggravated bull in my face, huffing and puffing around the topic of body image. I could feel he was extremely agitated, and I felt as though he represented the opinions I had endured from others. For example, when I was in the sixth grade, one of my friends said to our group of girlfriends, did you know if you can grab an inch of skin on your stomach, you are fat? There I stood, the only one among us who could grab an entire inch, and I was called fat. A member of my family made a comment once where I was eating very little, and this person said, "Elizabeth does not eat that much, I don't know how she got so big." Big being 5'7" and 130 pounds. Then there was everything behind being a cheerleader in high school, the stories go on and on. I have gone to extremes to be a size 8 simply because I have allowed, and continue to allow, the opinions of others and societal standards to take over. When I am at a size 8, I then desire to be smaller. It is a vicious cycle where I know genetic predisposition, environmental factors and life experiences all play a role.

With all that I have endured, the intrusive bull had to represent the opinions of others, but as I looked the bull in the eye, I knew there was more to his significance. I allowed in feelings of empowerment which led to giving myself a saddle to put on the bull. It was at this moment, I realized the bull represented my entire being, from my mental state to my physical state, the bull was my mind. I have lived in a state of aggravation for so long, it was literally breathing into my face because this topic is so up close and personal, it was essentially a part of me. OK then, let's saddle this. I put the saddle on the bull and got on, and there I was in a true leap, plunge and spin, holding on for dear life. Making every attempt to stay mounted, so much so, my body began to feel out of whack. The bull became exhausted, and so did I. He gave up and I gave up, simultaneously, the two of us were in sync. I see both of us lying down, allowing for sacred rest.

My mind is tired of this topic, so damn tired. I have literally worn myself out thinking about what food I should eat, the amount of water I should drink, the exercise I should be doing, and even saying no to events out of fear of weight gain and judgment.

I lay there and began to look around and realize that the bull and I were in an arena, one big fucking arena, where the spectators, like the bull, are my thoughts and emotions. This made so much sense because my life at times does feel like one big rodeo where my thoughts are the ticket holders and I am in the center of it all, being judged. I look at the VIP section and see guilt, shame, embarrassment, and even disgust sitting in the front row. I feel the rope in my hand and I masterfully lasso the adverse feelings up and swing them to the cheap seats up high and in the back. Years ago, I would have most likely had them ushered out, but I don't see all negative emotions as bad, they serve me because when they show up, I simply know I have something I need to soften. I feel better wrangling them to the back and this is a tribute to my personal growth.

I felt strong at this moment. This life of mine is indeed my fucking rodeo, and I am "steering" this journey with my thoughts.

I lay there and think about what thoughts I want to be VIPs: thoughts that give me feelings of empowerment, love, ease, joy, and flow. I continue to lay there and then remember another bull in my life that I was introduced to while reading my son the story, Ferdinand the Bull by Munro Leaf. Ferdinand the Bull would rather smell the flowers than fight in bullfights, when faced with actually having to enter a bullfight, he finds absolute delight in the flowers being thrown at him by the female attendees. He sits down in the middle of the ring to enjoy the flowers, and as a result, he is sent back to pasture where he sits happily smelling flowers. I feel this, here he was the biggest bull in the land, but he stayed true to his desires and his large body, despite the opinions of others and who they thought he should be.

I allow thoughts to be delicately tossed at me like flowers from supportive spectators, I bask in this moment. Feelings of wellness and body aesthetics allow for enhanced thoughts of appreciation towards my body. I have carried two children, I have run marathons, I do yoga, and the most beautiful flower of all, I woke up today. I am still here because my mind, body, and spirit are in sync. My body is a beautiful vessel and it works for me, not against me. Like Ferdinand, I may be perceived as fierce because of my handling of situations, but at the end of the day, my highest desire is to sit under a tree, look at the flowers and appreciate my state of being. From the others, who are allowed into my arena, my highest desire is to only expect flowers, flowers in the form of supportive words and actions.

From this point forward, I give myself permission to rest, not because I have completely exhausted my mind with body loathing thoughts. The rest I give my body is in appreciation for all my body has done for me, it's time I give back to her, she has been through so much.

I feel the applause from the crowd, I feel the love, and I see the standing ovation. I am choosing flowers over bullfights, and my mind feels the ease of this, even my breathing feels different. I welcome all of this. I am my own bull-riding champion of my thoughts, I hold the record for being my greatest fan and this, in turn, changes who and what I allow into my mental arena. My life is a rodeo, and I am choosing to enjoy the ride and the rest *in a body that I love.*

As I close this meditation, I feel a new kind of peace behind the saying *Stop and Smell the Roses.*

Make sensations not sense. Again, life is a feeling journey.

1. What negative thoughts hold season passes in your mind, primarily, which ones are your VIP TICKET HOLDERS? They are sitting in the front row, allowing you to feel your physical body being judged. If there is a particular memory, give yourself permission to let it go.
2. Picture yourself throwing a lasso around a negative emotion that no longer fully serves your body image, what is an emotion that you can throw to the back of your mind? Explain. What is a thought that feels better about your body that you can have sitting in the front? How is your body image improved by allowing this positive emotion in?
3. Are you mentally exhausted? Are you allowing for daily sacred rest where you carve out time for yourself daily? If so, is it enough? If not, what can you do for yourself daily to allow for more ease, joy and flow?
4. Are you your greatest fan? Do you rely heavily on the opinions of others to dictate the opinion you have for yourself? If you are not your greatest fan, what gives you the feeling of being applauded? For example, what is something your body is really good at, and rest can be included (doing nothing is doing something). Who are the ideal people allowed into your life's arena when it comes to body image?
5. When, if ever, have you complimented and appreciated your body, take the time to do so now. What is a compliment you can offer your body, a thought that feels like a flower given from a place of appreciation?

People NONPleasing

Attraction Point to Ponder 14

My entire life I have been putting the needs of others in front of me. There is some childhood trauma behind this, all too often, growing up I didn't have my basic needs met nor did I often feel loved based on my own perceptions. I have spent my adult life making sure my loved ones never experienced lack in all areas.

Today, however, I woke up exhausted. The last two days have been spent assuring quality of life for everyone but myself. I look so forward to quieting my mind to soothe this, I live to go inward.

As I explore the idea of people-pleasing, I tend to see the overlap with my anxious and avoidant attachment style. I recall learning in Psychology 101 that people-pleasers try to earn love through self-sacrifice, and even though someone may be avoidant or anxious like me, there is still a need for human connection. When we think about attachment, it is rooted in an individual's core personal need for love and validation.

Having been raised in an environment offering inconsistent and unreliable love and security, I have learned to work around life's uncertainties by finding ways to deem myself worthy of secure connectedness with others. These self-validating behaviors show up when I unnecessarily go above and beyond for others, when I don't set healthy boundaries, and when I say yes when I actually am a no.

I value myself enough to remember I am a person also, and my primary relationship should be with me. As I begin my journey from powerlessness to empowerment by having the desire to be at the front of the line in my life, there is guilt.

Quieting my mind with guilt in full force, I immediately see a crow. Instantly I recall having a playground monitor at our elementary school who would tell us to be careful of crows. She would go on to say that crows actually hold grudges and they could remember a face.

This, by all means, was not the case, I didn't hold grudges, or did I? Or did people hold grudges towards me for not doing enough? Deep breaths and self-soothe, I tell myself. I begin to think of a recent walk I was on and saw a crow with a big crumb in its mouth. He looked like such a badass for his find, and this memory felt better. I feel like crows are not offered enough attention for how inquisitive and resourceful they are.

As I sit with the crow image, however, I begin to then think of the mightiest eagle and allow this to replace the crow. I think my discomfort with crow imagery comes from an analogy that I was exposed to as a school employee. As I once worked at a school where an EAGLE was the mascot, I recall we held a staff meeting and discussed how the broad wingspan of the eagle makes it so they can fly higher than crows. We used this analogy to illustrate how we can ignore the criticism and doubts of others. Fly higher than the crows the staff heard, just like an eagle.

I also think about the time I learned that eagles fly above storms instead of seeking shelter.

I allow myself to embody the eagle and soar above any meanings I give to other people's judgments of others for desiring to put myself first. I soar and soar and feel myself become a luxury jet. With such ease, I allow myself to feel like the pilot in my own cockpit. I place my family members in first class. I find great joy in assuring my loved ones that they experience comfort from being cozy, fed, and in terms of safety. I can't let this part of me go, nor do I desire to.

As I tune in, I receive a memory of my son as a baby, on a day I desired a hot shower. I carefully placed him in a bouncy seat in the bathroom with me, I buckled him in, I placed his favorite blankie on him, turned on the lighted toys and told him I loved him. I showered with the curtain slightly open so I could assure his safety and well-being while meeting my own needs at the same time. I loved this memory because it was an empowering visual of how I find pleasure in taking care of my loved ones but have a strong need to carve out moments for myself as well.

Coming back to my luxurious jetliner, I love the idea of having crew members, where I am actually asking for help with all that needs to happen for a successful life's flight. I appreciate this version of me, one who feels and appreciates the freedom of asking for assistance. I have always struggled in this area, and I am giving myself permission to let this go.

I leave the cockpit and come out to the main cabin and get on the speaker. I welcome everyone aboard my flight and let them know that the destination is towards my life's dreams. I make it very clear that I will not be taking any detours towards other people's desires, and I will not tolerate unruly passengers who present themselves with criticism towards me. Today, I am preparing for my life's take-off, and my new baseline is to be surrounded by supporters, so much so that any "baggage" on board actually gives the flight a beautiful distribution of weight, so my journey has true balance.

OH CAPTAIN, MY CAPTAIN, I think of the movie GOOD WILL HUNTING. I feel so empowered.

I communicate with the flight tower, I see this as the Universe, I share my desired destination and all that it entails. It feels so good to share my desire aloud with something that places the safety of all of us first. The flight tower is my path of least resistance, I know and trust the Universe to ensure a safe flight no matter what storm patterns I encounter.

Programming my life's flight panel with ease, joy and love, I prepare for take-off.

I reflect as I soar. Like an eagle, I have a strong desire to soar above the crap. I love the idea of having all of my passengers being taken care of, but it also feels good to also ask for help in my journey. This idea of having a helpful crew as a single mom is foreign to me but very welcoming. The feeling of making announcements is also so empowering, I love the idea of actually creating boundaries that assure a safe flight and landing towards my dreams. Most importantly, I love the idea of the Universe working behind the scenes in a flight tower, where all of my desires are backed by energies that are beautifully orchestrated for me. I simply have to be clear with my vision of where I desire to go and be ready for take-off with my own personal vibration.

In terms of my own life, I have come to the enlightening realization that, metaphorically speaking, I have been riding standby for too long. I have missed too many flights. I sat in the cheap seats. My destinations have been overlooked and ignored. I have allowed turbulence with my own worries and fears. I have even canceled many flights, rebooked them, only to cancel again.

So instead, I bask in this whole idea of preparing for take-off. Sitting back, communicating with the Universe, and then programming my desires in from a place of pure intentions with ease, joy and flow. Thanking everyone for flying with me, I assure my life's passengers we will arrive safely, and most important of all, I am staying the course towards my highest desires.

I am choosing to fly the friendly skies and that means choosing me. In any circumstance, you have to first breathe from your own oxygen mask first, only then can you truly help others.

1. Who in your life do you find joy, pure joy, in making them feel like FIRST CLASS PASSENGERS? Are there people that are part of your journey that you could actually seat in the main cabin? By that I mean they are in your life, but they do not have to be up close and personal.
2. If you were to get on a loudspeaker, as your life's pilot, and announce new boundaries for everyone, what would you say?
3. Knowing the Universe and God are safe to communicate with, what are the highest desires you have for YOU that you are willing to say aloud, knowing there will be no judgment?
4. Who are the people or resources around you that you can ask for help from? Are you willing to ask for help? If not, why?
5. Not one of us would transport our loved ones around while tired, what are you doing for sacred rest? Are you putting on your own oxygen mask before helping others? What could you do to change this?

Believing is Receiving

Attraction Point to Ponder 15

This is the year that I have decided I am going to show the Universe I am ready to receive. Full disclosure, I have never been good at receiving, this may be a self-worth issue, possibly backing

my feelings of inadequacies. There also may be a poverty mindset behind this where anytime I received I felt as though that money would be better spent on necessities.

Memories where I believed in Santa Claus are memories often free of guilt. I truly thought that no one was spending money on me and the toys were created in a North Pole workshop for me because I was a good child. With this, I received it all openly. As long as no money was spent and I was good, I was open to receiving.

This was recently put to the test by my inner being's very entertaining sense of humor. Only twenty days into the new year, I was invited to wine tasting with a friend and she offered to pay. I fought my urge to insist on paying for it all or at least paying for half. I had to consciously stop myself, and honestly, this felt like shit. This is one area I knew in my heart was worth exploring.

Initially, I thought my shame came from my marriage, where I was never on the same page financially with my former spouse. I always had guilt around receiving simply because of a dynamic within my marriage, and one I am willing to own. I own it because, after today's visual journey, I realize I came into marital life with residue from my childhood that was living within my inner and outer surface of my entire being. Closing my eyes, this journey began with a noise that somewhat startled me, it was the sound of my grandma's adding machine. We would visit her in the summer, and she owned one of these contraptions that were always sitting out with a full receipt roll loaded and ready for use. I loved seeing it as a toy where I could play office secretary. My grandmother, who grew up with food rations in England during World War 2, however, did not see it as a toy. It served her nickel and dime mentality where every penny spent was added together.

Suddenly flashes of things I heard growing up around raising kids began to play themselves aloud within my mind's mental loudspeaker. I can hear my grandma talking about the expense of having children, not only myself and my sister, but also her own four she raised. I can hear moms around me saying, "I won't be able to own anything nice until my children are 18, they take all my money." Sadly, I was also privy to a conversation where my mom told my dad that she is willing to freeze the amount of child support from increasing over the years as long as he commits to his monthly visitation schedule. I realize I have always felt like a financial burden. The root of my uneasiness around my ability to receive was completely tainted by the idea that having my basic needs met was already so expensive, so asking for anything more was shameful.

Needing to feel better immediately, I shift my thoughts to making the machine become a black plastic file folder holder, like one you would find in a workspace. This felt better but gave me feelings of a business transaction. I did love the idea of a pocket, nevertheless, that the holder had. I thought of things in my life that had pockets… my subconscious gave me a welcomed visual of me sitting in a classroom on Valentine's day.

On this particular Valentine's Day in mind, we had woven larger construction paper hearts, the colors were red and pink. We taped them on the front of our desks. I remember sitting in anticipation, so excited to hand valentines out and so excited to see my valentine holder full of cards and treats from my friends. I bask in this. I loved milking a delicious memory where my capacity to receive was so heightened with such innocent anticipation. I can remember my teacher saying this rule for Valentine's Day, "If you bring one Valentine for one, you bring one for all." Knowing this rule made it so I did not allow any lack of consciousness in, I was assured to receive one from everyone who participated. I see myself freely handing out my valentines while at the same time returning to my desk to see the full valentines pocket. I would open my valentines willingly, knowing they were all designed to be kind. All of my expectations felt so supported by pure intentions from everyone around me.

At this moment, I realized that my highest desire is to feel this daily, to simply allow the laws of the Universe to serve me by closing my void gaps around my receiving shame, and to widen my receiving container through excitement and certainty. I begin to feel the energetic movement within me as I allow my entire being to feel like a pocket aligning myself with being ready to hold all of my desires. My human pocket's inner lining felt ready and my outer lining felt ready.

I allow myself to float back in time with my entire being embodying a feeling of being a complete pocket worthy of receiving and being big enough to hold all of my desires. Once again, I hear the adult conversations around the costs behind having children, and I see this enlightened version of me effortlessly proclaim, "I AM WORTH IT. I AM FUCKING WORTH IT."

The release of these words feels so good, I realize I have never said these words aloud. As I see myself standing tall with these words, I then see myself in a random laundry room. I am cleaning out various pieces of clothing before they are washed. I see myself excited because I find coins and dollar bills. Realizing I am open and ready to receive from all areas of my life. I do not have to limit myself. I feel so much appreciation for my readiness to receive, whether it be expected or unexpected, my human pocket is so worthy of receiving. Releasing the old versions of me allows for this version of me where I am one big happy pocket full of sunshine.

May my light shine so bright so I attract others who join me in seeing my high worthiness of having all that I desire.

1. How are you at receiving? For example, if a friend calls and asks to take you out, are you open and ready, or do you feel guilty and not worthy? Explain.

2. Do you remember hearing any conversations as a child around money or any topic that made you feel like an emotional and/or financial burden? If so, how can you reframe it from a place of high self-worth? Have you ever proclaimed, "I am worthy!" How would it feel for you to say these words aloud?

3. What memory can you tap into where you were in the absolute receiving mode? Describe in detail what you were FEELING at this moment.

4. What do you bring to your relationships in terms of your readiness to receive? How would your loved ones describe your openness to receiving?

5. Are you calling abundance in? Do you limit your receiving opportunities to predictable modalities like a work salary? Explore possible unexpected ways you may receive from others, for example, a co-worker bringing you a coffee drink without you asking, or a fabulous savings find at a department store. List out playful possibilities.

Life is Delicious

Attraction Point to Ponder 16

As an adult, the theme of food being associated with massive weight gain has always been an issue for me. The other night we went to a restaurant known for its pizza, and as we entered, it had a very pre-covid vibe to it. The entire restaurant felt lively, people were truly enjoying a Friday night surrounded by great company and delicious food. We ordered my favorite pizza with ranch on the side. When I tell you this is the best pizza I have ever had, I mean it. I did psychologically well at dinner, I enjoyed my company, I enjoyed the atmosphere, but only for the most part, I enjoyed my delicious food. My goal, which truly comes from a place of effort, is to enjoy my food with guilt. I found my head saying the old story, "You shouldn't eat that, it has carbs, cheese, etc." I want to move through this so badly in my life, and as I write this, I realize how active my desperation vibe was. I allotted myself one and a half pieces and gave myself permission to eat the crust. The eating experience felt dictated by my irrational personal guidelines. As we went out to the parking lot, a car pulled up next to our car, and an enthusiastic couple got out. The man was thrilled, and so was his partner. He said, "We have been coming here once a week for 25 years, and I am so excited!" His positive energy was through the roof, here is a person entering a restaurant with such fun anticipation for what he is about to indulge in, and I, at that moment, realize I always enter restaurants giving my power away to setting the intention to watch what I eat. The interaction with this man felt life-changing. He looked like a champion of his own cause, a fighter in the food ring that was winning, and as for myself, I was losing the fight. I appreciated this stranger's presence, I know he was one of those agents sent to my life so I could feel the trigger of my own emotions. My eagerness to soften food guilt was activated.

When we got home, I closed my eyes and thought of the guilt, shame and envy that was sitting in my stomach with such heaviness. Immediately I had the vision of a large round piece of molding cheese just absolutely gut-bombing me. I love cheese, so immediately, I desired to see something better to avoid any aversions surfacing. As I embraced the roundness of its shape, I pictured a merry-go-round, the old metal one that was on my childhood neighborhood's playground. As I see the child version of me on the playground, the structure spinning, I feel dizzy. I am dizzy. I have been dizzy for so long with the topic of food. The desire to put my foot on the ground and stop this dizziness is there. I do just that, scraping my foot along the ground until the spinning stops. I desire for the entire Universe to witness me taking a physical hold of my food intake unsteadiness. The dizziness begins to subside but I still feel lightheaded.

I see the playground as a whole, kids playing and the adults sitting on the benches watching. I begin to think of my life with food as a child to my life with food as an adult. I am offered a fantastic memory where my best friend and I around the age of 9 would order pizza every Saturday night and watch Saturday Night Live. We would even eat popcorn and drink soda, and I would think nothing of it in terms of guilt. There was never any mention of calories or possible weight gain. We would both enjoy, laugh, and live in the moment. Life was so good. I began to think about my journey into adulthood and pictured myself in my dorm on a Saturday night, and we thought we were so cool because we had pizza delivered to our room. For the first time in my life, I witnessed other people take the cheese off their pizza to "cut fat," I saw people not eating pizza to "cut carbs," and then the ultimate, I heard someone say, "I don't eat pizza because I don't want to get fat." After this moment, I never ate pizza the same. I was reminded of my childhood struggles with weight. As always, I own my own story, and from a triggered state, I attached the pizza perceptions from others to my own pizza experiences. I sit here with feelings of shock over how easily I was impressed upon in my early adult years and the lingering effects all of this has had on me.

I pivot and return to the image of the playground again.

I recall the idea that "food is my friend." This saying had a very low vibe to me. Food is my friend, but more like a fair weather friend because during difficult times, food was there for me in an unhealthy fashion. For example, my need for food disappears when I am stressed, my desire for processed foods always increases after a shaky day at work, and at night, my cravings increase for all things crunchy and salty. So yes, food is my friend, but this saying, for me, invites the same ups and downs one might experience in an actual friendship.

I go back to the playground, and I hear, loud and clear, FOOD IS PLAY, EATING IS PLAYTIME! I felt ready to hear this. I think about the energy of play, it feels so free and cathartic. Allowing playful activities on any given day gives my life balance. FOOD IS PLAY, EATING IS PLAYTIME! I see myself on the playground running around, going to every play structure, and life feels amazing.

I then see myself as an adult version of myself sitting on the playground's bench. Whereas I do agree we are all observers of our own emotions, life as an adult just sitting and watching did not feel like a balanced life.

I begin to think of a balanced diet and the emphasis it places on nutrition. I am now rethinking this stance. Allowing the idea that a balanced diet is indeed about nutrition in terms of food, but it is also about soul nourishment as well. It does not feel playful at all to sit at a dining table with feelings of guilt and shame within you, this feels like a killjoy. What feels playful is the man in the parking lot who is celebrating his once a week rendezvous with pizza. He didn't accept the script of adulting that reads one must sit on the bench as an adult and just observe, or the page that reads, one should feel guilty for eating pizza. Yes, there is a time and place for this, but food is play. Play feels so full of freedom, and eating should as well.

With all of this comes a major epiphany for me, and I feel the energetic shifts immediately. For so long, I have attached meaning to food based on what others bring to the table in terms of their own thoughts. Watching television and eating pizza was exhilarating during one time of my life, but I instead chose to give more energy to the night where food had conditions. My desire to eat from a place of pleasure feels so damn good, I am open and ready to attach not new meaning to, but the meaning I once had as a young child to my food experiences. I smile to myself, picturing myself saying to the people in my life as I ask them to go eat with me, "Do you want to go on a food playdate with me?" These words are backed from a whimsical place in my soul that agrees: FOOD IS PLAY, EATING IS PLAYTIME! Everything about my life's menu suddenly feels like a 5-star restaurant dining experience, as it should.

I close this meditation and allow in delicious memories of a recent savory restaurant experience I had, and yet I now embrace that the delicious moments in life also occur when we simply choose, trust, and surrender. Decide. Simply decide.

1. What emotions do you bring to food? Be honest.
2. Think of a time when you thoroughly enjoyed food as a child. What were you eating? What were you doing? Who were you with? Most importantly, how were you feeling?
3. Do you have a moment in your life where your food script was flipped? Where did you hear a comment(s) that completely altered your perceptions of food? Who said it? What did you feel when you heard these words? Are these perceptions playing a role in your current reality?
4. As you nourish your body with food, what are you doing to nourish your soul in terms of offering your body balance…we all seem to easily embrace the serious side of adulting, but how are you balancing your soulful journey with play?
5. What new meanings can you give your food experiences? Let's take back our power. Take a moment to visualize yourself as an adult truly enjoying food. What you are feeling, how do you look, what are you eating, and now embody this version of yourself. From this embodied version of you, how might your life feel more delicious?

Keep Calm and Get Your Spa Day on

Attraction Point to Ponder 17

Continuing on with this year's theme of receiving by allowing myself to receive from a place of total appreciation and worthiness, I was given a day at the spa. This new version of me was not going to allow this certificate to gather dust so I booked the appointment immediately from a place of high self-worthiness. As I entered the incredibly inviting spa, the hostess explained to me that I would be wearing a shirt and shorts provided by the spa, and in the mandatory soak area, nudity was my only option.

Deep breaths as I processed being nude in front of other women.

As she handed over the perfectly folded towel, shirt, and shorts, I immediately saw the size of the shirt on the outside with the letter L plastered on the front. I was triggered. Instantly. Why did my thoughts suddenly go towards Hester Prynne from The Scarlet Letter, she wore an A for Adultery, and here I am about to wear an L for Large. There is a backstory here, even when I was at my lightest weight, the people in my life still bought me size L clothing and it always fed into my body distortions, there was always an assumption I would gain the weight back. Let me be clear, I find all body shapes beautiful, I just have lingering resentments from being gifted large clothing when I was actually losing weight rapidly as a cry for help. The large purchases made me feel ignored. So naturally, in total defense mode, I said aloud as she handed me my bundle, "I apologize, I am not a size Large." She then said, "Our clothing size is not measured by United States standards but by Asian standards, our large size is America's medium size." I felt embarrassed that I even questioned her professional judgment and I was embarrassed this was even an issue for me.

I also then remember in middle school, playing on a basketball team, and I dribbled the ball down the court. I knew, everybody knew, it was time to be fitted for a bra.

All I know is my mom took me to the closest department store, straight to the undergarments section, and this all felt like some backwards rite of passage. There the salesperson, with her bifocals resting on the end of her nose, measured my breasts with a soft measuring tape used for sewing. She had me lift my arms high in the area as she said my measurements aloud, I was mortified. I had grossly underestimated the size of my breasts, and society and bras would offer true and realistic numbers. Needless to say, the idea of body measurement has always been a topic of discomfort for me.

I remember being angry at the clothing industry for existing, like statisticians who all believe anything in life can only exist if it is measured.

The only thing that was worth measuring in my first bra moment was my level of shame not cup size.

Despite the spa attendant's matter-of-fact explanation, I just couldn't get over the L being broadcasted on the front of the shirt and the reasoning behind it. Coming from a place of compassion and logical reasoning, I can only imagine that having the size on the shirt's front served the person folding the clothing in terms of organization. Deep breaths. My logical mind was still being consumed by my illogical self.

In full monty, I apprehensively soaked in the hot bath area and then went to the Rock Salt Room to meditate. As I quieted my mind, I began to think about the letter L for large on the front of my shirt. I was offered a memory from my university's Social Psychology class, where my professor asked us to draw the fruit we felt represented our bodies. We were exploring self-perception of body size disturbances and body dissatisfaction and how they possibly lead to the development of eating disorders. I was completely fascinated to learn that body image includes both positive and negative self-perceptions and attitudes regarding the body…I had always assumed that it was only about the negatives.

For my body perception, I drew an upside down pear. Rounder up top with legs that were slimming. I saw this inverted pear in my now reality and asked Source to offer a better feeling fruit at this moment. To my surprise, I saw a banana. I always love my inner being's sense of humor and her entertainment level so I allow it. I knew the banana was not a reflection of my body, but my perceptions of my body. My fears felt a little silly as I thought of monkeys eating bananas, but the monkeys made me think more so of mimicry behavior.

So true, here I was once again, in my monkey mind mimicking thoughts from a low-vibing state versus thoughts from my quantum self. To truly embrace the new paradigm, I am reminded how my quantum self shows up in this world, owning my entire being, including my physical body and my emotional guidance from a higher sense of self. My quantum self is a badass and would let this shit go or let it serve her. Knowing this, my monkey mind needed to be soothed. I allowed my quantum self to see the size L for Large on my shirt. I asked her how the size L was perceived by her. "Size L for LARGE, LARGER THAN LIFE THAT IS." The message I heard was immediate and clear. Again, I was reminded that I was attaching meaning to my own perceptions of what LARGE means, and I thought about what LARGER THAN LIFE meant from the frequency of who I desire to be. It was at that moment I felt immediately compelled to regain myself as one who lives largely by following her paths of highest excitement, I am reminded this is my path of least resistance. Body distortions are resistance, body acceptance is allowance. Sometimes we have to remember and it is my dominant intent to remember to feel good from a place of total appreciation, awareness, and alignment. This is what it means for me to live LARGE.

I basked in this and was offered a vision of Laverne from Laverne and Shirley, a 70's sitcom that I adored growing up. I think about the cursive L that was a signature on all of Laverne's shirts. Going by Liz growing up, I would take black markers and draw *Ls* on many of my shirts. Lots of wow factors as I recall how I used to rock the letter L on my shirts, and today I allowed myself to go down the emotional scale with feelings of shame. L was for LIZ when I was growing up, and I would wear my shirts with confidence. Never did I think about someone associating the L with anything but Liz, and by all means, never with the word large. I tap into my childlike innocence where the L represents me and pair it with living larger than life as my version 2.0. I air write a cursive letter L, the kinesthetic experience of this is pleasing. Why did I allow life to change what L meant for me personally? I release this question and allow for my life's circumstances to serve me. Somewhere in my journey, I had made a choice to redefine what wearing an L meant for me, but it does not have to be an eternal choice. I hold the marker, I always have, and my marker is washable, not permanently based on my personal evolution. I sit here in peace, knowing my reality is my canvas from my t-shirts to my thoughts, and I am my reality's artist.

I come back into my physical body and I allow this energetic shift to move through my body. I stand, shoulders back, and allow this aligned state of being to own the idea of a big L on my shirt. The meaning I personally attach to the L from a place of unconditional love is more powerful than any meaning the people around me offer from a place of judgment. I hum the Laverne and Shirley lyrics ``Making Our Dreams Come True" as I walk around the spa, "We're gonna make it, give us any chance we'll take it, read us any rule we'll break it…We're gonna make our dreams come true, doing it our way." My spiritual team and I are definitely going to do our way…we are choosing my new life's story from my higher state of being, this is the unabridged version of me, feeling larger than life emotionally and spiritually. By doing so, I feel more complete with being unapologetically me from head to toe.

1. Would you be openly willing to wear a shirt with the letter L on the front? Why or why not, explain. If you were to wear a single letter on your shirt that represents you in some way, what would the letter be, and what would it stand for? Would your letter selection be in total agreement with your higher self?

2. If you saw someone with an L on their shirt, what are your honest perceptions of what the L means? Does your definition come from a place of judgment or acceptance? Sometimes our perceptions are mirroring a perception we hold for ourselves, exploring this in detail.

3. What is something you did as a child that made you feel good about yourself but maybe now, as an adult, you no longer partake? What is getting in your way, are there particular emotions, be specific.

4. The Monkey Mind is a state of being unsettled or confused; is there a particular thought about you that feels restless? For example, as the thought passes through your mind, you find yourself distracted, almost as if you are jumping from place to place in your head. What can you do to ease this?

5. Do you walk around with your shoulders back and your head high? Describe the version of you that is most confident. What makes you feel larger than life? What can you do to feel like this more often? Tap into your quantum/higher self for your responses.

Manic Manifesting

Attraction Point to Ponder 18

When it comes to manifesting, sometimes I feel like I do all the things. I journal, meditate, exercise, do yoga, pivot my thoughts to better feeling thoughts, and the list goes on. Yet, in my physical reality, there exists some sort of block with bringing my materialistic manifestations into reality. Simply by stating this, I become immediately aware I am giving energy to the problem. Part of me truly believes that manifestations are old news. I say that because I have come so far with my own self-soothing where I am truly showing up in this life so much happier but if thoughts become things, what is inhibiting my power to bring wealth in, the car, the house, etc.? By simply having this question, I can feel my split energy, as I describe it, I feel like I have one foot on the dock and one foot on the boat when it comes to manifesting.

I quiet my mind as this is all activated with me, and I see a pair of scissors cutting up my new year's intentions I had journaled. Realizing at this moment that there was a part of me that feels like setting intentions is a waste of time because I don't see concrete evidence of the material bounty I desire. Doubt is definitely the emotion behind all of this. Startled by feelings of doubt, I find myself questioning everything, and then reminding myself that the LAW OF ATTRACTION IS A LAW, like the LAW of GRAVITY, it is a universal law. I think of the scissors and ask my inner being to offer something to me that feels better, and there I see crochet needles. Trust me when I say I do not crochet, but holding the needles steady feels better than using a pair of scissors to cut up my scribed dreams. Initially, the crochet needles bring me thoughts of the FATES in Greek Mythology.

The Fates were a feared personification of destiny, of the three women, they all carried their respective tools to represent their part in determining one's fate. They are three sisters who spin and measure out the destinies of man. In many recounts, the three sisters were stubborn, strict, and unchanging. They know everyone's past and future. They assign to every person as they spin and measure out the individual destinies. They know everyone's past and future.

The Three Fates are described like this:

Clotho is the spinner of the life thread, often depicted with a spindle.

Lachesis measures the thread and is often depicted with a staff.

Atropos means the inevitable and is the cutter of the thread and was often depicted with a pair of scissors or shears.

I know I am not willing to accept my fate being in the hands of others, although I have my doubts as a creator, I still embrace my power to create.

I then allow crocheting memories to flood in, going back in time, I picture my mom on our 1970's couch, creating the quintessential orange, brown and cream blanket that so many of us seemed to have back in the day. Coming back to the present day, I think of my daughter with her natural ability to watch a how-to crochet video resulting in production of beautiful crocheted stuffed animals. I continue to think of my daughter and her gifts. She is currently taking ceramics, and she comes home with the most incredible pieces she creates, from vases to sculptures. Her gifts as an artist are beyond admirable. I then begin to think of my son, and I think about how he is not an artist per se, but his gifts include the ability to code on a computer. He can program for himself and others a technological experience that offers ease and flow. My mom, my daughter and son are all magnificent creators. I think of my own ability to create, in terms of a hobby and I feel let down. I found this moment to be very eye-opening, I don't think I realized how deep my doubts around my ability to create ran so deep. I see creators all around me, but I lack consciousness when it comes to my own sense of creativity. As always, my inner being responds from a place of unconditional love. Allowing myself to receive images of myself as a creative creator led me to see myself in the kitchen. This felt amazing, because I love to cook. Creating in the kitchen brings me so much joy, and I am a gadget junkie, I thrive using various utensils. The kitchen version of me should have naturally occurred when thinking about myself as a creator, obviously there are blocks, and unlocking them is a level up moment for me. I am a creator, yet until this moment, I don't think I have really internalized this. In the kitchen I truly believe that any meal is possible and that all of my tools used for preparation are appreciated. I sprinkle in a little of this, and a little of that, I pride myself on not being a recipe reader but as someone who measures with her heart. I believe in the outcome of my meals no matter what, because if the meal turns out poorly, I ask myself, "How could I make this better?" Alternatively, if the meal turns out delicious, I still wonder, "How could I make this even better?" I cook in a state of playful curiosity, I get so excited, wondering how everyone will react and how the meal will actually look and taste. Everything about cooking for me is delicious, pun intended, because no matter what, I cannot get it wrong. As Abraham Hicks says, "There is nothing really serious going on here." I don't prepare a meal, thinking I will not be happy until this meal is done to my standards, the kitchen is a place of play for me, I thoroughly enjoy my food preparation processes. I begin to see myself as a creator. When I cook, I am not at all attached to the outcome because I am always open to better and my cooking journey is so fulfilling.

I know this applies to manifestation as well. It is not only about being detached to any outcome, it is about allowing joy in the journey. We are iron chefs in the creation process, not recipe readers. Some manifestation recipes tell us to do exact things, to be calculated, by offering so many modalities like affirmations, setting intentions, angel numbers, moon mantras, etc. When we manifest from a place of effort, however, by doing exactly what we are told to do, we are possibly activating feelings of desperation, lack, and doubt. When we are being completely bonded to a specific outcome, we are limiting possibilities for ourselves. I cook with playful curiosity, I vibe with my love for food and my family, I embrace the journey as my own. Manifestation is very similar, from the viewpoint offered by the highest intelligence, it is a feeling journey where you bring in playful curiosity towards limitless possibilities. Even on your best days, even with your best meals, we should feel empowered to ask, "How can this be better?" All while knowing the better it gets, the better it gets. Opening ourselves to so many likelihoods expands our container as a receiver. We are iron chefs in this journey, because we play with ingredients that bring us personal joy, we don't have to follow other people's manifestation recipes.

I close this meditative journey with a vision of Julia Child's saying, "To be a good cook you have to have a love of the good... and a love of creating." As I toast this meditative meal, and I say a toast to myself, "Cheers to finding joy in the journey, cheers to having playful curiosity, cheers to being open to personal possibilities, and cheers to knowing the secret sauce in life are ingredients YOU find pleasurable." Bon Appetit!

I come back into my awakened state, knowing that total indulgence is ours to have, we all exist as creators. This life is meant to be a 5-star dining experience where we sit at the table of life in excitement and curiosity of what is coming. When we cease being our own hasty critics with our doubts and poor reviews, and give ourselves thoughts and emotions that completely satiate our whole being, then material manifestations become irrelevant.

1. Do you have a specific modality you are dedicated to when manifesting? Do you have faith it is working, elaborate on this. What is the evidence of its effectiveness in your physical reality?

2. Who are you as a creator? Describe an area where you see yourself as a creator in your physical reality.

3. Are you open to the idea of being the creator of your own destiny through your vibration or do you find comfort in turning your destiny over to an alternate power?

4. When you set an intention for something you desire, do you find joy in the journey, or do you need that desire to happen before you can experience joy? Elaborate.

5. What ingredients in life bring you pleasure? Once you make your list, now make a grocery list of other ingredients, _manifestations_, you would love to phone in. Activate feelings of joyful curiosity by deactivating the need to know how they will appear and any attachment to outcomes. We phone in reservations, we complete online take-out orders, we order coffee drinks with amazing detail, take this time to request your desires, writing them down in detail with the purest intentions and harm to none. Knowing that manifestation is a feeling journey, how would having each desire make you feel? Are you open to feeling these emotions as often as possible in your current reality?

Your Fuck-it List

Attraction Point to Ponder 19

Prince was found dead at his Paisley Park estate on April 21, 2016.

When I read these words across the internet, that moment made me rethink my entire existence. Many lifetimes ago, I had made a BUCKET LIST and number one on my list was seeing Prince in concert, and now he had passed. I had allowed time and excuses to get in the way of making a personal dream come true. I was never going to allow my dreams to slip by again, and so I thought. My new number one bucket list item was to be a contestant on Wheel of Fortune. True Story. I had once heard that there were local tryouts in the town I was living in, but I learned after the fact, so I missed it. Then about three years ago, I learned that the WHEELMO-BILE, the show's mobile bus that allowed contestants to audition locally, was stationed in a city 45 minutes from where I was. When we went to drive to the auditions, the traffic in Seattle was so congested that the 45-minute trip was timed out to be roughly three hours. After about an hour of being stuck on the highway, we got off the freeway ramp and went home. For the record, I have lived with so many regrets around this decision.

As I think of this, I think of myself as being very guilty of skipping to the endings in life. I am always skipping to the endings, I even do this with the shows I am binging. I ignore the warnings of SPOILER ALERTS and keep reading. I should be using my energy to enjoy the show, not my energy to skip the show altogether just so I can fast forward through life.

I do not want to skip to the end of the story of my own life. I have spent so much of my life counting the minutes as opposed to making the moments count, and I do not have any SPOILER ALERTS here… I know how this will end if I don't start living according to myself.

I do not want to skip my ending so much that I don't at least try for WHEEL OF FORTUNE. I am alive, dammit. No more getting in my own way.

With all of this, then the pandemic hit. Our entire world began rethinking how they were doing things, even the producers and casting directors of WHEEL OF FORTUNE. The show announced online tryouts. I once again entered excuse-making mode, I was now turning 50, I felt like pandemic pounds and no longer getting Botox had impacted my image. I became worried about my online presentation. In awareness of all of this being a low-vibe state, I allowed for an appreciation of the show to step in. Submitting a recorded audition was the path of least resistance, there would be no traffic and no missed opportunities. I knew in my heart that my story was worth telling. I had stuttered miserably as a latchkey child back in the 80s. During my time home alone, I would watch the contestants on Wheel of Fortune as they pronounced words, and my attention paid off. Eventually, I was able to ease my way into the proper pronunciation of letters, words, and phrases. Behind my desire to be on the show lived a desire to pay homage to a show that changed my life. I felt like my story was worth sharing. Thinking back to Prince's passing, thinking towards getting my power back from my insecurities, I decided it was time to submit my audition virtually.

I go on the website and it reads:

We Want YOU!

YES!! OF COURSE, IT READS THEY WANT ME!!! OF COURSE!! I think about the idea of how the Universe offers us all the opportunities, but we are responsible for the outcomes. My vibration was completely on board with the idea of their casting team desiring my presence. I keep reading through the tryout information:

If you're selected, we'll contact you to set up a virtual audition from the comfort of your own home. Doesn't get much easier than that!

YES!! I thought I welcomed the ease of the process. This is all speaking to me. I keep reading.

Here's your chance to charm us! Try to follow these tips when creating your video.

- Choose a place where you can speak up and act natural.
- Don't record it in your office cubicle.
- Don't look like you've just rolled out of bed.
- Smile.
- Be natural.
- Tell us something interesting about yourself.
- Tell us why you'd be a good contestant.
- *Don't tell us that being on Wheel is on your bucket list.*
- Don't ramble.
- Less is more.
- Keep your video under one minute.
- HAVE FUN!

I found myself thinking about the fact they didn't want to know this was not only on my bucket list, it was number one on my bucket list. I knew this was a sign to own my story. I was being guided by the Universe. Had the suggestions not mentioned the BUCKET LIST no-no, I would have opened with an emphasis on mine. These guidelines were guidance, and I was on board.

From a place of excitement and appreciation, I submit my one minute video. I made the video with a one and done mentality, zero fucks given, just submit and allow the Universe to beautifully orchestrate this coming to fruition. I then detach from any outcome, I bask in my taking steps towards my dream, and play pretend as if I was watching each show while embodying myself as a contestant.

Many weeks later, I saw a woman win BIG on the show, and Pat Sajak asked, "How long have you been trying to get on the show?" She responded, "THIRTY YEARS!" I seriously thought, "What in the actual fuck?" I then googled and discovered that it can take up to TWO YEARS after your audition for the show to actually appear on the show. Disappointment took over my body. Why did I wait so long to try out? Why do I always get in my own way of allowing my desires in? I sent every signal to Pat Sajak to not retire until I was on the show. My highest childhood desire was to meet both Vanna and Pat.

Nevertheless, feelings of disappointment overwhelmed me. The idea of allowing for divine timing was not enough for me to get over my self-inflicted blocks. Here I am, believing in limitless living, but I am guilty of not always following inspired impulses, and by doing so, I found myself in a waiting game. I pray that the 75-year-old Pat Sajak does not retire as the show's host because Prince didn't live long enough for me to follow my inspired nudges to see him in person.

Sidenote: *This whole time I am assuming I will be selected because my desire to be chosen surmounts any fear of not. At least I had that going for me.*

There's my bucket list backstory, it was time for me to ease the disappointment and possibly some fear that comes with a waiting game.

I picture myself in my own bed and begin to think about the disappointment Goldilocks feels as she attempts to rest in the first 2 of 3 beds in the story Goldilocks and the three bears:

Now, being determined to rest, Goldilocks went upstairs into the bed-chamber in which the Three Bears slept. And first, she lay down upon the bed of the Great Big Bear, but that was too high at the head for her. And next, she lay down upon the bed of the Middle-sized Bear, and that was too high at the foot for her. And then she lay down upon the bed of the Little Wee Bear, and that was neither too high at the head nor at the foot, but just right. So she covered herself up comfortably and lay there till she fell fast asleep.

She also experiences trial and error with the porridge and her chair selection; also, everything had to be "just right" in order for her to commit to her selection. I don't want this to be my story, I realize I am open to allowing for discomfort if it means making a desired dream state come to reality. At this moment, I am thinking that I often wait until everything is "just right" before I make my move and with this visualization, I am willing to let this go. This download speaks to me and I am open to receiving it.

I felt there was more, I then saw LITTLE RED RIDING HOOD, and I sensed this had to do with time, the little girl being a young version of me, the forest's path being the trajectory of my life, grandma being the old version of me, and the wolf being the excuses I make when it comes to experiencing my own joy. I think of the wolf saying, "Well," said the wolf, "and I'll go and see her too. I'll go this way and you go that way, and we shall see who will be there first." If the wolf represented my excuses, then he was indeed almost always arriving first.

What I don't want is for my life to pass me by, and I miss my path. I then think of the wolf's reply when Little Red Riding Hood comments on his teeth, "All the better to eat you up with." And, saying these words, this wicked wolf fell upon Little Red Riding Hood and ate her all up. My excuses tend to eat me up, but so does this idea I have around time. Intellectually, I am reminded that I simply see time as a construct, and there is no way I am going to live disappointed for the next two years as I wait for my opportunity to be on the show.

It came down to this, during my journeys towards my desired life, it is not about having everything "just right". Life is about going down the path, living aware of the wolves showing up figuratively in our lives as excuses, and not allowing so much time to go by that we end up ultimately missing out on the adventure. I reframed my disappointment with a Hansel and Gretel mindset, I was going to begin to allow for incremental thinking, leave bread crumbs along the way towards all of my dreams so if ever I get off my path, I would be able to get right back on my path. I no longer want to feel lost, detoured, or misguided. My dreams are many, and my breadcrumbs are left by setting intentions, visualizing my desired life, and choosing joy. I allow this in: Enjoy the journey, live aware of emotional hazards behind excuse-making and disappointment, and stay on the path by being intentional with your thoughts, feelings and emotions. At this moment, I realize that so many of the fairy tales I grew up with all came with shocking and sad endings. We have Goldilocks that escaped into the forest, we have the wolf that ate Little Red Riding Hood, and we have the witch who pushed Hansel and Gretel into the oven. Not all fairy tales have happy endings, and obviously many of them end in darkness. I, however, have a core belief that in darkness there is light, and my fairy tale will come with not only a happy ending but with beautiful beginnings throughout. Through my vibration, I create the happy ending where I live happily ever after, and after that, I continue to live happily ever after, and so on and so on. Time is simply an illusion. Life's happy endings can happen daily by living in appreciation of what is vs. being dependent on the occurrence of an event to happen.

The ultimate download is here: BE YOUR OWN BUCKET LIST.

As my grown children have said to me, YOU DO YOU,

One may not be comfortable believing everything in this world IS POSSI-BLE, this may feel exhausting and unattainable, causing split energy. Instead, live in the impossible, where impossible is I'M POSSIBLE. I AM POSSIBLE: What I desire is based on my own standards, not the standards of others or society, go for the fucking life that feels good to you. Fuck it! Like Goldilocks, live life not too little, not too much, but just right... for YOU.

1. Do you have a bucket list? Are you successful in completing items on your list? Yes or no, explain.

2. What excuses do you present yourself with that prevent you from achieving any of your dreams? Do you have to wait until everything is just right, why or why not?

3. How can you transform your dreams into reality by being more intentional? What incremental steps can you start taking towards your dreams, what is doable so you can stay on your desired path?

4. How do you view time? Do you allow for the divine timing of events to beautifully unfold, or do you have a sense of urgency or a notable vibration of impatience? Feel what impatience feels like in your body and now explore how patience feels. Impatience can create resistance. Explore this.

5. For your highest desire, think about the feelings you would experience by having that manifestation occur, can you allow this feeling or feelings into your new reality? Do you find joy in the journey, or are you dependent on certain occurrences to happen in order to feel good?

Rainbows among the Clouds

Attraction Point to Ponder 20

I have a strong tendency to be easily overwhelmed when I am faced with stressful situations, especially ones concerning finances. This feeling today was so activated in me, and I know so many can relate to this.

Whether or not I have money, I have this lingering fear that it will go away. For example, even if I have way more than enough money in my checking account, when I swipe my debit card at the grocery store I fear it will be declined. Other times, I worry that when I have a plethora of money, something catastrophic will happen and it will all be dissolved. Even when I am frivolous financially, I worry that some sort of karma will come after me teaching me not to be reckless with money. I have so many money wounds that still need to be healed, so my money story isn't on repeat.

As always, my inner being has a strong desire to feel better. I know that when I feel like crap about a situation, it is because my inner being does not agree with the matter at hand. There exists a solution that comes from unconditional love for me and today I desire access to it. Sometimes simply having a lack of clarity is something to soothe, especially around money matters.

I close my eyes and immediately see myself in a cage, holding on to the bars and looking out. It is dark and gray and lonely. Deep breaths, I remind myself I am never truly alone. This feels a little better. I know I have my spiritual team, and I know I have God. I am not alone.

Reminding myself that I am a powerful creator who is supported, I see the cage's bars as malleable.

I am. I create.

Figuratively speaking, I am the molder of my own clay. Allowing myself to be guided from a place of unconditional love, I take 7 of the metal bars and bend them into a rainbow shape. I see each bar as one of the colors on the rainbow: RED, ORANGE, YELLOW, GREEN, BLUE, INDIGO, VIOLET.

I still feel some doubt as I think of the saying, "Life is not full of unicorns and rainbows." As one who is committed to challenging my limiting beliefs with a viewpoint from my higher self, I counter this by leveling up with the phrase, "There's always a rainbow after the rain." At this point, once again, I remember to remember. For every storm that I have weathered in my life, there have always existed feelings of peace afterwards. Thoughts of seeing a rainbow after a sizable storm allow me to feel present, to feel encouraged and to know that something better is coming my way. I allow myself to live in an appreciation of what rainbows represent to my whole being and how so many benefit at even the sight of one. It is at this moment, I realize that whether or not the rainbows are seen or unseen by the human eye, I know rainbows still exist after storms. This idea applies to my manifestations, I know I do not have to actually see them to believe they are there. I can feel good knowing they are coming. It is done. I must add there is nothing more satisfying than unexpectedly coming into the complete view of a rainbow, this is a feeling of total abundance for me. As I look at a rainbow, I am able to beautifully tap into source consciousness. I am reminded that I am an extension of source energy, it flows to me and through me. My love for the rain compounds this moment of appreciation as I think about the feeling of freshness all around me after rain showers. Feeling all of the tingles with this, my highest desire is to feel fresh vs. feeling stressed. When I feel fresh, I feel cleansed both mentally and physically, and this offers me a total state of clarity. I allow for guidance from a place of clarity. The message I receive is, "Always allow light in through what is cracking you apart." I think of all of the states of being I am in when I am cracking apart, I feel like I am breaking down, bursting at the seams, exploding, and most of all, like I am shattering.

I definitely see myself shattered in moments of stress. Here I am beautifully reminded of Kintsugi: The Centuries-Old Art of Repairing Broken Pottery with Gold.

Poetically translated to "golden joinery," Kintsugi, or Kintsukuroi, is the centuries-old Japanese art of fixing broken pottery. Rather than rejoin ceramic pieces with a camouflaged adhesive, the Kintsugi technique employs a special tree sap lacquer dusted with powdered gold, silver, or platinum. Once completed, beautiful seams of gold glint in the conspicuous cracks of ceramic wares, giving a one-of-a-kind appearance to each "repaired" piece.

This unique method celebrates each artifact's unique history by emphasizing its fractures and breaks instead of hiding or disguising them. In fact, Kintsugi often makes the repaired piece even more beautiful than the original, revitalizing it with a new look and giving it a second life.

I see my financial scars concerning my childhood, my marriage, and my single mamahood be filled in with gold. I feel stronger. During my childhood, I felt ashamed asking for anything new. During my marriage, I spent uncontrollably self-medicating my personal misery, and as a single mom, I spoiled my two children to compensate for the dissolved marriage between their parents.

I now truly embody the idea of allowing my cracks to be filled with gold while also allowing cracks of light into my physical world when I am struggling. Taking myself out of a cage into a world of nature where bits of light are shining through during a storm offers so much relief.

Still puzzled a bit, I hear my own voice ask, "In times of stress, how can I let more light in?" My inner child, whom I cherish, reminds me of my love for the game CANDYLAND. I think of the spaces on the board, and of course, they are all mainly the colors of the rainbow. Reflecting on my need to pick my favorite colored gingerbread man game piece, and now knowing it is not the color of the game piece that matters, but who I am vibrationally. I bask in the memory of moving forward among the spaces. There always exists the possibility of getting stuck and losing a turn on one of the licorice spaces, but I still desired to always move forward. I regress to a childlike state and feel my love for board games, especially this one. Just like I did when I was a child, I know I can allow for the stressful situations of adulting to be opportunities to move forward, space by space. Seeking beautiful shortcuts out, like Gumdrop Pass or Rainbow Trail, along with knowing the possibilities of temporarily feeling stuck, still offer playful curiosities towards the desired outcome. In the new paradigm, very similar to this particular game, there is really nothing I have to fix, solve, or figure out. The focus of any game should be play, and like life, it is meant to be experienced with joy. I can always move forward with the guidance of the cards, the cards being the signs around me and within me that I am on the right path. I can always move forward following inspired impulses. In this life, I know I am being guided along a rainbow path where my emotions are an indicator of whether or not I am moving towards all that I desire. My life, like Candyland, can feel like a sweet adventure if I allow it to be.

I close out this meditation by thinking of the game Candyland and its simplicity. There is no reading involved, and even when I feel stuck, or when I am losing a turn, delicious experiences still await. I realize it's time for more simplicity, time to move forward one space at a time, time to allow for more inner guidance, time to let more light in, time to give beauty to my wounds, time to weather any storm knowing a rainbow awaits and time to allow for lighthearted possibilities in this game we call life. In closing, while playing Candyland, I felt like I could never get it wrong, and this was a reminder to me that even in moments when I don't feel like I am on the right path, I am still on the right path. None of us can get it wrong in the new paradigm where contrast serves us as we live life on the leading edge of empowerment. I am always on the right path and I am reminded that manifestation is a feeling journey, where the path is colored according to our thoughts and emotions. A candy castle awaits all of us and we can all see how a rainbow symbolizes rebirth... we simply have to decide to play by facilitating our own freedoms from thoughts that imprison us.

It is not about limitless possibilities, the winning space seems to be more about the selected things that I feel are possible by my own colorful standards, not societies nor the people in my life.

1. When you think of finances, what is the first emotion that surfaces? Is it a positive or negative emotion, explain in detail. How would you rather feel? Level up no matter what your response is.
2. What thoughts imprison you? What are better feeling thoughts that you can allow in through the cracks?
3. What is a limiting belief you have about yourself or towards difficult times? Challenge it from your higher self and share the transformative thought.
4. As you move through life's journey, are you allowing for inner guidance? For example, if you are stuck, or lose a turn, are you able to use this time to serve you by quieting your mind and allowing yourself to be tuned in? Or do you allow for the inverse, when you are stuck, you simply feel stuck and that takes over? What is one way you can move forward through your life's stressors by at least one space?
5. What could give beauty to your scars, whether they are emotional or physical, or both?

Shake It Off

Attraction Point to Ponder 21

There are a few topics in my life where I present myself with a sense of urgency. When I feel urgency within me, I feel anxious and overwhelmed. There is a strong side of me that feels like I am always in trouble, so when I think of possible outcomes, I tend to see something bad happening to me in the end. I believe I have certain life events that feed this feeling, mainly stemming from being such a *good girl* growing up, that when I did mess up, any small deal was made out to be a big deal. As a result, I can easily allow certain topics to completely consume my thoughts with phrases like, "Let's just get this over with!" or "I wish this was all behind me." These phrases are not from a place of impatience but rather from a place of believing that some sort of punishment will happen no matter what, so just bring it on now.

On this particular day, I have been in my head since 5 o'clock this morning. Typically, I love to wake up and immediately have amazing feelings swirl through my head all the way to my toes. I typically tap into memories where I felt peace, and juice those memories for about 5-10 minutes every day. This sets a nice tone for the remainder of my day. This morning, however, I was paralyzed by thoughts concerning two circumstances

I want to be over. It is at times like this I take my own personal thoughts personally. Going into deep breaths, and going into my subconscious mind, immediately, I saw my own hands folding a paper airplane. There was such precision with every fold and every crease. In some ways, this reminded me of the anxious feelings I have always carried with me. I didn't fold my paper airplanes to be exact for accuracy or for aesthetics, I folded them with total fear of, "What if my plane is the only plane that doesn't fly?" My fear of failure has always been with me.

I shift thoughts with the intent to feel better, I then see my hands playing with an EtchaSketch. An Etch A Sketch has a thick, flat gray screen in a red plastic frame. There are two white knobs on the front of the frame in the lower corners. Twisting the knobs moves a stylus that creates line graphic images. The one aspect of this toy that I so appreciated was when I made a mistake, with a simple shake, the slate was cleared, and I could start over. The opportunity to renew at any given moment was empowering, knowing I could simply shake it all off.

As I continued to look at my hands, I began to make shadow puppets with them. On the wall, I could see the shadow of a butterfly. I allowed myself to use my hands and imagine the butterfly flying across the wall. I can recall being in my bedroom all by myself as a little girl, waking up scared and making shadow puppets on the wall to ease my fears until the morning came.

Now seeing what appeared to be three uncorrelated images of the paper airplane, the EtchaSketch and the shadow butterfly, this is when I asked for the message.

LOUD AND CLEAR, I heard, "Time flies when you are having fun." This phrase struck me with great intensity, not only could I not remember the last time I had heard it, or spoke it, I also could not remember the last time I had fun. This epiphany was heavy for me. What had happened in my adult life where fun was no longer a priority? I immediately set an intention to have more fun. As I relax into the idea of having more fun, I see myself as a little girl road tripping to my grandparent's home. It was less than a three hour drive, but in my mind, it felt like an eternity. As cliche as this sounds, I would constantly ask, "Are we there yet?" and my mom would respond, "Why don't you look out the window or something?" In the 70's, I didn't have any electronics, we were too poor. I can remember desperately wanting a yellow walkman, but always knowing the financial means to get one did not exist. As I have learned to solve problems on my own as an adult, it is in these moments I am reminded that I also learned to solve my problems on my own as a child. I now picture myself packing my road trip bag with my coloring book, crayons, reading books, and of course, my EtchaSketch. I had learned to create my own sense of fun on road trips so the journey's timespan would go by faster. I began to truly encompass this feeling of creating fun for myself.

Thinking back to the last time I truly had "fun", I could not recall any moments of true laughter and total enjoyment. Looking forward to my life, I had recently received tickets to see Chelsea Handler, an American comedian, actress, writer, television host, and producer. We would soon be going to see her in person, as well as going to cocktails with my best girlfriend. I think of Chelsea saying, *"Laugh loudly, laugh often, and most importantly, laugh at yourself."* Here I sit, realizing I don't remember the last time I truly laughed loudly, and truly I don't laugh often enough, and I don't laugh at myself. As I thought about going to this event, it was with curious anticipation I couldn't wait but I also could wait. I have within me such an amazing confidence that my evening is going to be a total blast so all is well. This confidence felt heightened even more so now that I was deliberately setting the intention of having more fun and with Chelsea's presence I had total certainty.

Although I felt like I had digressed, I am realizing two very profound thoughts for myself. As a child, I created my own fun during long journeys or on scary nights, and this gave me the feeling of being present with the gift of feeling like time flew by even when I felt a sense of urgency. I choose to be present now, but with certain urgent matters, I can get off the topic by simply creating fun. In addition, I am realizing when I have an upcoming event that in my head I know will be fun, I look forward to it with total excitement. It feels very empowering to see all events with total excitement towards any outcome knowing everything is always working out for me. Had Chelsea's show happened before this meditation, I think more of my thoughts would have been on seeing Chelsea in person, and now more of my thoughts are on allowing more fun in. Figuratively speaking, I hold my life's EtchaSketch in my hand and in my mind at all times, I am a powerful creator. I don't have to create with such precision and worry, I can create knowing I can't get it wrong. I can literally SHAKE IT OFF. I hear myself proclaim, "Have fun loudly, have fun often, and most importantly, have fun with yourself." The Universe is my wingperson, she is by my side, I simply need to romanticize my life within my rekindled relationship with fun. No matter the event or the outcome, the Universe will have me in just the right place at just the right time.

I now come with an awareness that even in my darkest times, I can still make paper airplanes and shadow butterflies, knowing time flies when I am having fun, I just simply need to get off the opposing topic. Within me, I always have the ability to pivot my thoughts through self-entertainment. Enjoying this road trip we call life is what it is all about. Looking out the car window of my soul, my urgency is soothed, knowing enough time has passed, not trusting how things will unfold. I no longer need time or anything else in my life to be folded with precision, I can trust my flight pattern, my overall journey, and how it will all land. It is time to allow for the divine folding *and unfolding* of events.

I close this meditation by sitting with the image of a butterfly flying erratically, I once learned they bob and weave on purpose. The erratic flight pattern of a butterfly makes it difficult to be caught. I feel now that the butterflies I feel in my stomach during anxious times can exist outside of me from a place of being an observer of my own reality. My lens can choose to focus on the fun in my funks. I am reminded there is so much beauty to be seen in our current moments and to allow the unpredictability by not getting caught, so to speak, by my own negative thoughts.

1. When was the last time you had fun and laughed? What does fun feel like in your body? How can you tap into the feeling of fun more often?

2. As a child, what problem did you have to solve on your own? Do you find this memory to be empowering? Share in detail on why or why not. Explain how you can begin allowing or further allow this to serve you as an adult.

3. If indeed time flies when having fun, how can you be more present in your life by bringing more fun in? _It is not about time flying by, it is about finding joy in the journey._

4. When you think of possible outcomes in your life, do you know everything will always work out for you? How can you double up on this certainty? Or do you have a little bit of doom and gloom, like possibly you may get into trouble or something bad is going to happen? If so, are you open to setting intentions for any outcome knowing the Universe has your back? Explore this.

5. What do you do to SHAKE IT OFF when you are way too much in your head? Explain how you can SHAKE IT OFF more by giving zero fucks?

We are Union Strong

Attraction Point to Ponder 22

I grew up in a union family. My father was a bread delivery man at PIKE PLACE MARKET in Seattle, WA, and my mother would later work for BOEING. She landed the BOEING position after many years working in a plastics factory with low pay and long hours. As a child, many of my family discussions were about the importance of union membership in a workplace. The conversations varied from insurance plans to overtime pay, being thankful for lunch breaks, paid time off, and especially a forty hour work week. It felt natural, yet unnatural, for me to seek out a profession where I would be protected by a union.

At this very moment, I have a very distinct memory of watching the movie *Norma Rae in 1979* with my newly single mother. My mom went from being a married stay at home mom to a mom who worked in a factory very similar to Norma Rae.

The film is based on the true story of Crystal Lee Sutton which was told in the 1975 book *Crystal Lee, a Woman of Inheritance*. The film follows Norma Rae Webster, a factory worker with little formal education in North Carolina who becomes involved in trade union activities at the textile factory where she works after her and her co-workers' health is compromised due to poor working conditions. I can recall looking at Norma Rae and how tired she looked and thinking the same about my mom and dad, despite their union memberships. I always lived in appreciation of the union, because if my parents looked exhausted with a union backing, what would they be like without one?

At a young age, I had somehow internalized the idea that, unlike my parents, if I went to college, being part of a union would not be so exhausting. In my mind, a profession backed by a formal education would leave me less weary at the end of a work day. Reverting to type by doing what I thought I was supposed to do, I can remember the day I signed onto the teacher's union. By agreeing to monthly membership dues for the teacher's local and state union, I had pleased my parents at least. In my mind, at the time, that is why I thought we were all here…to carry on the legacies our families had instilled in us. Parent Pleasing: Pleasing your parents despite what it means for your own happiness.

Tragically, even as an educator, yet a union member, I felt out of alignment. In union meetings, I would witness the leaders and members tirelessly represent themselves, and always felt so fortunate to be a member of one. Yet even with all of the contractual protections, so much is still demanded from employees. Despite all the fine details of our union contract, my advanced education, and my love for teaching, I was still depleted. I had become the exact image of my bone-tired parents.

Fast forward many years later, as turning fifty approached, I realized that despite my union memberships within my career, now having been on both sides of the table as a teacher and administrator, I had not pursued my very personal lifetime dream of becoming a published author. To be blunt, I had lived to make everyone else happy but myself. Of course, my light shined as an educator and a parent, but I knew my light would shine even brighter as an author, an uplifter, and public speaker.

I lived with my highest desire being to now live my truth. One year ago, I made the decision to step away from my career and pursue my dreams. Throughout this last year, I have experienced moments of shame with the people closest to me questioning and judging my decision. The SHAME GAME where I am a pawn on a very public gameboard and my opponents are all members of society. In all honesty, I felt like a loser for not working as I followed my path of highest desires.

Disappointing the people in my life for leaving a union profession is extremely active within me, and one I should have eased many moons ago. I closed my eyes and within moments I saw a wooden coffin and a hammer and a nail. My initial thought was that by quitting my job, maybe I literally put a nail in my own coffin. As if walking away from a union job was the ultimate death wish. This felt dark, claustrophobic, frightening, dirty and lonely. This visual also served as true testimony of how drastic my thoughts around this topic had become.

I also thought about the quote I would hear growing up, *If Your Only Tool Is a Hammer Then Every Problem Looks Like a Nail.* Maybe the Universe was telling me to put more tools in my toolbox, and maybe I was seeing everything around me as a problem and not a solution.

Focusing on, "How can I feel better?" I knew at this point anything would feel better, and I was allowed in a visual of a bed of roses and I laid on it in exhaustion. I then tap into a memory of one of my parents saying, "Life isn't supposed to feel like a bed of roses, Elizabeth." I have a distinct memory of agreeing to this statement on the outside with a nod, but my inner voice proclaimed, "Yes, it is." Recalling this, I choose to own this moment, it is mine to experience as I wish. In a state of appreciation, I laid on a mental bed of roses and it felt very childlike. I still see the hammer and nail laying to the side of me, and I replace them with a pen and journal. Playing peekaboo with the sky and giggling to myself, I begin to make shapes out of the clouds. As the clouds come together, I see a big puffy heart. I can feel how deeply supported I am by the Universe to create the life I desire. Daydreaming is where all of my creative energy has always resided, my imagination is an innovative canvas for my life. Feelings of abundance always fill my consciousness when I create images in my mind, and this heart cloud is a preamble of the love I have for pursuing my dreams. I allow these feelings to fill my consciousness, and I see the heart cloud slowly move as I totally relax. A reminder to me that everything I have dreamed about for my life originated in my mind; everything begins with a thought. I have so much love for this moment and, as I begin to be totally tapped in, I begin to receive divine downloads.

As I open up through this dream state, I feel so relaxed, calm and confident. What I try not to do is become suddenly startled when I receive a juicy download because this will disrupt the flow. The art of allowing means total flow of free consciousness for me. This particular message however spoke volumes to my soul and I wanted to jump for joy because it felt like freedom but I remained calm as I heard: YOU ALREADY HAVE A UNION CONTRACT WITH THE UNIONverse, the Universe offers you a spiritual contract through UNIONity CONSCIOUSNESS. I was like, drop the microphone, this was all I needed to hear. Immediately, I felt a transmutation of energy throughout every molecule of my body. When I think of unity consciousness, I feel this high level of vibration that reaches all beings through a sense of oneness, compassion, and unconditional love. This download completely offered total clarity.

Continuing on, I realize I am my own union representative with the Universe. I am already a member where I do not have to pay monetary membership fees, I belong by tending to my vibration, and living in alignment with my desires. There are no adversarial negotiations within my spiritual contract, there are actually open lines of communication where unconditional love is the dominant force. When I am in a negative emotional state, this is an absolute indicator that my inner being is in vibrational discord with the matter at hand. The purity of my soul occurs when I experience emotions that bring me feelings of contentment, love and joy. The more in tune, the more I am aligned with my inner consciousness. I embrace the knowingness that I am protected, and as I have evolved, my spiritual contracts have evolved with me. There is a new and welcomed awareness that I have always been a member of a cosmic union, one that is larger than all of us. We are indeed all connected within this vast Universe.

I see myself holding a strike sign walking through the blocks of my life, and my signs openly state my aspirations and I hear: *As you declare your written desires, hold the signs steady with your vibration, and we will give you the signs that you are on the right path.* I acknowledge that signs are indeed all around me in the form of abundance, I just have to be in the receiving mode. Abundance is my birthright. I also feel empowered knowing I don't have to share my highest desires with everyone; I can hold my written signs high, or I can hold them low. I can also choose to simply share them only with people who will support me. Communication with the Universe is the key and I am doing that all of the time with my emotions, thoughts and feelings.

Contrary to the opinion of others, this past year, I have been more energetically productive and creative than ever because I am honoring my spiritual contract with the Universe. I continue to bask in knowing my agreements with my inner being are spiritually irrevocable and the benefits are ever-lasting. My Unionverse membership has always been honored and always will be. The Universe is also an equal opportunity employer, meaning it pledges to not discriminate against anyone based on race, color, religion, sex, national origin, age, disability or genetic information. The Universe does not unjustly treat humans differently; we are all included and honored within our own journeys, desires and happiness. WE ARE ALL MEMBERS of the same union.

I close out this meditation thinking of the award-winning song in Norma Rae by Jennifer Warnes titled "It Goes Like It Goes". The lyrics:

> ***Bless the child of the workin' man***
> ***She knows too soon who she is***
> ***And bless the hands of a workin' man***
> ***He knows his soul is his***

Our soul contracts are personal, there is no need for any banishment, only acceptance, and there should only be love and no judgment. What served my parents on their journey, or anyone else, does not have to be what serves me in mine. I picture Norma Rae holding a sign that reads: UNION, I sit with an image of me proudly holding a sign that reads: UNIVERSE. With these downloads, I feel totally complete. We all are one, we are all connected, we are all represented, and we are all protected. I feel the strongest sense of unity behind this new awareness as I embrace my union membership with others, my inner being, and the Universe. The more replenished I have become, the more my inspired impulses are heard and followed. I have shifted from exhaustion to exhilaration by honoring my own spiritual contract and this one is eternally binding.

Be unified from within.

1. Did you pursue your own life's dreams… are you living out the dreams pressed upon you by the opinions of others, or are you following your inspired impulses? Share in detail.
2. What gives you feelings of being safe and protected in general? Do these feelings come from within, or do you solely depend on external factors? What can you do to enhance your internal resources?
3. Take the time to daydream and create your desired life from a childlike and rested state. If you truly embodied your highest desires, what would actually be happening in your life personally and professionally?
4. Do you judge others for their choices, if so, could this be a reflection of a perspective you are choosing to practice for yourself? When people share with you their desires, do you respond with love and acceptance or judgment and banishment? What does unconditional love mean to you?
5. Do you have people in your life you can openly share your desires with? If so, who are they, and what do they offer to you that makes sharing your desires an open exchange? If you don't have people to share with, how can you "hold up your written signs" representing your desires to the Universe? Focus on when and how to maintain vibrational steadiness for yourself. Meditation? Journaling? Daydreaming? Embrace a daily practice that connects you to the Universe at the emotional and visceral level.

The Story of My Life

Attraction Point to Ponder 23

As part of my morning ritual, I visualize and feel into my desired life. One of my powerful daydreams is becoming an author. I love picturing myself at book signings, I love picturing books written by me at local bookstores or amazon, and I love the thought of being stopped in public and someone sharing with me that my book changed their life. I can easily bask in famous author imagery and feel all the feels.

Scrolling through social media today, I came across a statistic that read: 85% of people desire to write a book and only 3% will actually do so. Many start writing a book but never actually get published, and the fire in my author's belly burns so strong my goal is to never have it extinguished. Every ounce of my soul craves to be published. I could feel doubt take over as I ran these discouraging stats through my mind. Once again, I was on that mental hamster wheel and I was hell bent to get off immediately. Running circles in my thoughts were the what ifs: What if I am part of the 85 percent that simply have the desire to write but never follow through with being published? What if within the 3% I would never be included? What if I could never find someone willing to publish my writing? What if I die before ever seeing one book written by me to completion? Here is the comical part. I am at least intellectually aware that you can't take statistical facts, I use the word fact loosely, which you see on social media. Nevertheless, there still existed the *what ifs*.

Whether or not you desire to be an author, this meditation is about pursuing your life's dream.

Quieting my mind, within moments, I saw ice cubes rubbing together and melting. I think of the idea that I simply need to chill out when it comes to this topic. Deep breaths in, deep breaths out. As a psychology major, way back in the day, I can recall studying dream interpretation. I remember learning that *If you dream about melting ice cubes, it typically represents that emotions will arise that you need to control before they come out of hand*. Truly, this is one topic I wanted to maintain momentum in a positive direction. Stay cool, I tell myself, allow feelings of being cooled off to take over your body. Be cool. Feel cool. I welcomed this higher state of being, there is great power when we are able to simply chill out, relax and just be.

In my mind, I continue to look around the room in what appears to be a kitchen and I see a single bouquet on a window sill. Most of the flowers were no longer alive, there were flowers drooping and wilting, but some were still thriving. I just stared at it. The bouquet itself seemed to be made up of random flowers, all types and all colors. What mainly caught my eye was the muckiness of the water and the few flowers that were still spry. I found myself thinking about all of the bouquets I had ever received and there always appeared to be a few flowers that outlive the bunch. Never had I questioned this phenomenon before. My response would be to sometimes simply throw the entire bunch away when most of them had wilted. Other times, I sifted and sorted through them all and salvaged ones that were still flourishing. If the flowers held great sentimental value, I have been known to press them between the pages of my favorite book. Now, however, at this moment, I am questioning why some thrive longer while others do not survive for very long. I knew this imagery would give me answers to my desired outcome of becoming an author in spite of some made up or factual statistics.

I continue to stare at the vase of flowers and am very aware that the prospering flowers have received more sunlight than others simply because of their placement. In my journey towards being published, I began to think of ways I could allow more light into my life. I take a deep breath in and exhale. Allowing more sun rays into my life, figuratively speaking, also meant surrounding myself with others and circumstances that shine with me and for me. Another sifting and sorting process, as I think about who and what I want, and who and what I do not want in my life from a place of prioritizing self-preservation. I know I have things and people I allow myself to wilt with, and through further exploration, I own how this impacts my free flow. I have family members who I allow to make me feel like I am a dying flower. In their presence, I visually sag and sink, and I know this weakens my entire state of being. In addition, I have circumstances in my life that wither away at my ability to stand tall. Regaining my own power in this moment so I thrive towards my dreams, I commit to saying no to uncomfortable people, places, and things.

This awareness is compounded by how without question I always cut the stems of my flowers to prevent my blooms from drooping prematurely. Pondering how I could cut from my life the things that bring me weariness, I am reminded to give myself permission to let go of all that is no longer serving me. I can hear and read and feel discouraging words, but I do not have to receive them. Through my own personal preparation, however, I know that creating my reality is more than simply snipping off negativity. What we resist, persists. Carl Jung's famous saying that 'what you resist' persists supports the idea that our attempts to avoid something often gives it the energy it needs to expand.

> If you focus upon whatever you want, you will attract whatever you want.
> If you focus upon the lack of what you want, you will attract more of the lack.
>
> — Abraham Hicks

Law of Attraction says that what I mainly focus my attention on, will return to me in the form of more experiences that will match that same frequency I am emitting. Do I want to give energy and focus to the people who were never published or to the ones that successfully were? I accept that I must be deliberate and intentional in what I absorb from and emit to my outside and inner world. I am choosing to grow with a focus on what I want versus what I don't want.

Now shifting to a focus on nourishment to allow for me to thrive, I find myself thinking about the murky water. Am I drinking enough fresh water? Or am I putting so much crap in my body that it stifles my creativity by making me tired or less focused? This was when I had to get real with myself. I love red wine. I love an occasional soda. I love flavored drinks. By all means, there was room for more clean and pure water. Stay hydrated, a simple message, yet so vital towards one's vitality.

I then think about how genetics impacts all of us, even flowers, and I remind myself that I believe in mind over body. This was a powerful cue to stay in the vibration of wellness over illness. The goal in maintaining good health is to see the we in wellness and thank all of my amazing cells for working in such harmony towards my daily health. I have so much appreciation for my overall well-being and my being well.

Realizing there are so many ways to prolong the life of a bouquet, it comes down to proper care and being in the receptive mode. There are flower care recommendations, and there are self care recommendations. Some flowers actually live longer with the use of soda, vodka, aspirins and even hair spray. As with humans, there is no room for judgment. No matter the individual secret sauce, or in this case, the flower food packet ingredients, it is vital that you find the recipe that feels good to you. Whatever happens to those that desire to be published is irrelevant to me, to be one that defeats the odds means proper self care. Proper self care, in this case, means daily healthy nourishment, allowing more light in, surrounding yourself with encourages not discourages, allowing healthy habits to dominate, relaxing, hydration, and knowing we can alter some of our genetic predispositions with our mind. Nurturing our spirit, mind and body is this triangulation that leads to publication of any of our dreams.

Suddenly I became very aware of the divine download concerning this topic. It does not matter what is happening to the flowers around me, the flowers being other "budding" authors. My receiving mode, my level of proper self care and nourishment, and my faith in the divine timing of the Universe will prevail me. THE UNIVERSE ALWAYS PROVIDES, and I must do my part by being open to providing for myself emotionally, physically and spiritually.

From the teachers of the Law of Attraction, I also know that one seed planted from a place of alignment will produce a bounty that will outgrow and outlast any seed planted out of alignment. Alignment is the key. Tending to my vibrational garden keeps me connected to a place where my inspired impulses are received readily so writing occurs effortlessly.

I begin to close out this meditation, knowing what I desire is mine, and I cannot be taken off my path because of what others have experienced in a similar journey. Life moments are not fueled by miracles, as the product Miracle Gro might suggest to the gardeners of our world. The LAW OF ATTRACTION is logical and natural; it is a law. To bloom where I am planted means to nourish my soul through steady alignment despite what others are doing and saying around me and despite the statistics. I can also bloom with autonomy, I don't have to stay put. I now choose to be the flower that thrives and survives while pursuing her passions. As I live aware of my own space consciousness in a vase full of other authors, I sense my own presence as one with universal presence. It is within this essence of being, I can tune into accomplished authors by bringing forth the awareness: if they can do it, so can I. I will continue to blossom, knowing if it is to be, it is up to me. Embracing my flower as the interpreter of my vibrational reality, I know I can be both eternal and physical at the same time.

As I look around once more, I now see a universal vase calmly resting on the leading edge and the difference among each flower represents not that of personal history but that of personal expansion. There is so much beauty in this transformative moment, and I close by acknowledging and appreciating the totality of my radiant existence.

1. Have you ever heard something or read something that has derailed you from pursuing your life's dream? Why did you give your power away? How can you take your power back?
2. Is self-care a priority? Why or why not? How are you nourishing your spirit, mind and body? Are there any daily habits that could enhance your journey?
3. What do you do for self-preservation?
4. Do you recall something you created from a total place of alignment, where it felt effortless and free-flowing? Go into detail with all of the specifics. What can you do to allow more of these moments into your existence?
5. Give yourself permission slips to let go of the people, places and things that are wilting your soul's flower. What ingredients do you need from the world around you in order to feel supported and loved unconditionally?

Ages and Stages

Attraction Point to Ponder 24

As I think about being in my fifties, I reflect on myself sitting in a parking lot at the age of twenty-five and I heard someone on the radio say, "You will never be as young as you are right now." At that moment I looked at myself in the rearview mirror and told myself that I was not going to allow time to slip past me, yet here I was feeling like I did. With so many life experiences now behind me as I have raised two beautiful children, been divorced, moved back to my hometown, deaths of loved ones, and the list goes on… time propelled right on over me. Some days not only do I feel weary, I also look weary. I don't want to feel like I am invisible, yet I feel invisible. All of this is the antithesis of my highest desires of now wanting to be seen as an uplifter, a spiritual entrepreneur, and truly showing up in my life. I still embrace being in the land of the living, and there is a big part of me that feels like I am just getting started. Having split energy however on what it means to be in my prime may disrupt my beacon's frequency, so I am truly motivated to bring comfort to this.

As I close my eyes, I feel more reflective than relaxed. I think back to my childhood, my teen years, my early twenties, the years of raising children, and to my current reality. There is a sense of sadness there. I am tired in both a good way and a bad way. My two children are my touchstones, I could not be more proud, and every sleepless night and moment devoted to them was well worth it. There are also some life circumstances that offer so much personal expansion. However, I can recall when I was in the eye of life's storms, I was completely wiped out both emotionally and physically.

My mind keeps drifting back to my childhood bedroom. The sense of sadness is now completely activated as I see myself alone in her bed and crying. The struggle was fucking real. I can feel tears in real time as I stare at a nine-year-old version of myself. I want to hug her and tell her she will be ok. I think about my life around this time. My parents had recently divorced, my mom was forced to enter the workplace, and my elementary school had closed due to structural integrity concerns. Laying on the bed next to nine year old me and holding her hand so she could feel my strength. At this moment, I had no words, I just wanted her to feel my appreciation for her bravery. She has always offered my life so much courage from a place of service and determination.

Looking around the room, I saw my bedroom dresser, it was cream with three drawers on both sides. I remember thinking it was the nicest thing I owned as I recall memories of myself hiding my journal within it, my maxi pads, and the notes passed to me at school. This thought is disrupted as I then see my mom come in and put my clothes away and leave, no exchange with me.

My inner voice gently says, "Clean your drawers out." The voice was loving and there was a sense of guidance.

The last thing I wanted to do was leave the side of the nine-year-old version of me, but I felt very inspired to listen.

I begin opening the drawers and putting items that no longer fit me to the side. If the item had a stain or hole, I threw them in the garbage. I offer appreciation to everything I keep and everything I dispose of.

I then close all of the drawers. They close with ease because they are less congested with unnecessary things.

A soft voice whispers, "Organize your items, fold them, straighten them out, give your drawers a sense of order." There was such attention towards me not feeling like I was in trouble. I then do my best, knowing my best is always my best.

Then in the most loving voice, "In life, choose only what is fitting for you." Again, attention was obviously being paid towards the sensitive presence of my inner child.

I think about the drawers of my thoughts and what needs cleaning out, what needs order, and what could I straighten out. The days of the adults in my life putting untidy thoughts in my mental drawers can be behind me. I now decide what goes into and stays in my mental drawers. I am the keeper of my own mental dresser, I put away what I choose to put away, I keep what I choose to keep. The order I bring to all my thoughts is up to my response to them.

We always think about the comfort level of the clothing we buy, but we should also think about the comfort level of our thoughts. When it comes to our bedroom drawers and closet, would we put clothes away that visibly cause us discomfort? This applies to our thoughts as well. Why would we put away thoughts that cause us discomfort?

What is becoming very apparent to me is the necessity of cleaning out the drawers of our emotions, thoughts, and feelings. What fits us at one time in our life may now fit us differently or may not even fit us at all anymore. We have to straighten whatever is messy within us.

I can't go buy a new dress and expect to permanently feel better. I have to first deal with what no longer fits me on the inside in order to feel better on the outside.

I then hear: *Aging is an adornment.*

I had never heard this before. But as I thought of the word adornment, my mind defined it as anything that accents attractiveness. Adornment is the frills, the garnishments, and the embellishments used to enhance the appearance of ourselves. I think of jewelry, accessories, makeup, piercings, fingernail polish, makeup.

Aging is an adornment. I begin to think of adornment as a process. The process of how we choose to be decorated not only externally but internally. How can we adorn our thoughts? I sense that it does not have to be this amazing makeover experience where we completely glam up everything. You can't put makeup on a pig, as my mother would say, because it is still a pig. Spiritually bypassing is not allowed.

I ask again, "How can we adorn our thoughts?"

I hear, "Have an authentic process that accentuates what you are thinking to a better feeling place." There are so many processes out there: journaling, having a life coach, professional therapist, yoga, rigorous exercise, affirmations. You simply have to adorn your life with processes that are a vibrational match to you. Most importantly, with or without processes, we can all allow better thoughts that allow us to feel better. For me personally, I meditate, journal, walk, have an alignment partner, a life coach, and read. I have a myriad of decorative modalities that enhance my inner and outer appearance, including my commitment to feeling better with my thoughts.

Your inner and outer being is attractive, no matter your age, if you choose it to be. Just like when you select accessories for your outfits, select accessories for your thoughts on how you see yourself from a place of appreciation. For example, the lines on your face are the embellishments from the laughter of the good times and the contrast from the perceived bad times. You would not want to erase all of what has served you, and they have both served you equally. Appreciate your lines, they tell a story, and we all choose what meaning we want to give them.

We deem our own *face value.*

I begin internalizing that there is spring cleaning of our thoughts that should not happen once a year but daily. Some thoughts may even be better served in the current moment by pivoting through naps, meditation or simply getting off the topic.

We put *tops* on our bodies for various reasons and occasions, as well as we put *topics* on our minds for various reasons and occasions. Ultimately, the goal for both should be comfort as opposed to discomfort.

I then experience a complete rampage of the following:

If you are uncomfortable with an outfit, you change it.
If you are uncomfortable with a thought, you change it.
If a drawer is messy, clean it out and tidy it up.
If a thought is messy, clean it out and tidy it up.
If you want to beautifully accentuate an outfit, you accessorize it further.
If you want to beautifully accentuate a thought, you accessorize it further.
If a clothing item is no longer fitting for you, you give it away, modify it, or throw it out.
If a thought is no longer fitting for you, you give it away, modify it, or throw it out.
If you feel fabulous when you wear an outfit, appreciate it.
If you feel a fabulous thought, appreciate it.
If you can clutter a drawer, you can declutter it.
If you can clutter your mind, you can declutter it.
If a drawer is disorganized, you can organize it.
If your thoughts are disorganized, you can organize them.

THERE ARE ALWAYS MESSAGES IN YOUR MESSES!

When we get dressed, we should feel good on the inside and out. Feeling good on the inside allows for more ease, and this will appear in one's appearance.

We are not aging, we are staging. As when a home is for sale, we clean it, add new decor, we light candles, play music, have vases with fresh flowers. Yet, as people walk through the home, they can still feel the home's vibration. As for ourselves, we can stage ourselves with jewelry, lipstick, etc., but to complete the outfit, one must live aware of the practiced vibration that is being presented.

My download levels up as my thoughts level up.

The vibration you practice towards aging is the ultimate adornment.

I love the idea of offering my inner child an adult version of me that is committed to keeping my thoughts in order and one who appreciates her courage and bravery along the way. I picture myself cleaning out my mental drawers, making room for more acknowledgements. We are still here, and this deserves to be celebrated in how I show up in this world. We have come too far to play small. Knowing where I have been, where I am now, and where I am going, I allow for my vibrational adornment to be laced with love, joy, and appreciation.

I close out this meditation and go straight to a mirror. I think of a nine-year-old me on that bed, I think of the 25-year-old me sitting in the car that day, and I think of me today. Taking on the role of an observer, I think of all of the positive aspects of my physical features. I say to myself, "I love you, I always have, and I always will." There is not a moment of vanity but a moment of raw humility. As I feel my words at the visceral level, I feel lighter and more attractive, both inside and out. Again, I am reminded I may never be as young as I am at this moment in terms of time passing by, but my personal vibration is timeless. My legacy will not be remembered for how I aged but for my vibrational offerings within our physical world. With a playful wink to my image in the mirror, I embrace myself as a spiritual being having a human experience. As pure non-physical energy before I was born into this physical body, I am reminded I am here for joy. I feel settled with relaxed expectations for what the wrinkles in time here on earth will bring from this point forward.

1. Are your mental drawers messy? What process can you use to clean them up? What are some ways you feel inspired to declutter your thoughts?
2. Do you live in appreciation of the times in your life when there was contrast? Allow for transformative thoughts towards your most dominant contrasting moment, write a statement about how this occurrence served you towards personal expansion.
3. What age of your inner child would you like to offer strength to and why? Go back in time and give this version of you a hug or hold hands, tell this version of you that everything is going to be ok and offer appreciation for being brave and strong.
4. Look in the mirror and spend time appreciating who you are both inside and out. Say _I love you_ to yourself. Share thoughts about what you see from a total place of acknowledgement for who you are.
5. What can you do daily to enhance and accessorize the thoughts that may represent a low vibe state? What is your pivoting technique? If you do not have one, what is a method you can begin to practice to get out of your mental body? What processes for self-betterment speak to you?

Constructive CRITICSism

Attraction Point to Ponder 25

I felt inspired to dabble with the idea of being published, my highest desire was to begin to embody the idea of being an author. Since my senior year in high school, I have launched many rockets towards being published for children's books as well as adult self-help books. Starting with kindle downloadable books seemed like an effective place for me to begin embodying being an author. As my uploads all moved to the status of being LIVE on AMAZON, I realized that all of the books lent themselves to be reviewed. I thought of star ratings, I thought of the comment section, and I began to also have word-of-mouth concerns. What ratings would I receive? What would the comment section read? If someone shared their reading experience with another person, what would they say?

Fear of criticism... I have personally come so far, yet here it was, rearing its ugly head within a publishing moment that was meant to be glorious.

Sleeping only 5 hours last night, I awoke with a certain level of disappointment in myself for allowing a dark cloud of fear to rain on my dream coming true parade. The disappointment was compounded by fear of critical words from the world's critics.

As always, as my wobbles are active, so is my imagination. What I appreciate in the moment is how quickly my mind, my inner being, delivers imagery. As I closed my eyes, I saw a taxi cab, which appeared to represent an UBER. I began thinking about ordering an UBER, the app allows me to share my desired location and, in return, offers my current location. I see myself using the app and getting into an UBER, taking all recommended safety precautions. There was a quick downloadable message here that I allowed, when we get into an UBER, we expect to arrive at our designated destination and we expect the journey to be pleasant. I embrace this as an affirmation fitting for me: I expect to arrive at my designated destination and I expect the journey to be pleasant.

As always, I knew there were more messages coming.

A couple of things happen in my mind as we go on our journey. The driver alerted me in a calm manner that he was low on gas, so he was going to stop and fill the tank. In my meditative state, there was no sense of urgency, so I was literally on board with him doing so. If this was a moment for an analogy to be made, it seemed too simplistic, if one's mental gas tank is empty, we should fill it. Maybe I was supposed to be open about the need to fill my own spiritual tank in life, but that didn't truly resonate with me either. Self-care is a high priority for me and one I do not need to justify. I can also recall Abraham Hicks sharing how we don't just simply place a happy face sticker on a gas tank and expect the car to keep running, nor do we sit at a gas station crying because our tank is empty, we simply fill it. At this moment, I appreciate remembering to monitor if I am running on fumes to take the time to replenish and rejuvenate with ease. Great reminder, but my fear of being criticized was still active.

We begin driving again. As he refers to the GLOBAL POSITIONING SYSTEM, he receives an alert that there is major congestion, and we are rerouted. Like my driver, I completely rely on my internal GPS system to navigate me, and my emotions are my guideposts. Oh yes, and another friendly reminder that if our mental state is congested, we can reroute as well. Rerouting, like pivoting, can simply mean getting on a different path by altering our thoughts to a better feeling place. I definitely had mental congestion today, so I began rerouting with the WHAT IF game. What if my books receive high ratings? What if the comment section is filled with acknowledgements and appreciations? What if people recommend the books to friends?

As I eased my mind, I saw myself looking out the car window. I am reminded of a saying I once heard concerning worrying: Worrying is using your imagination to create the unwanted. Time to reroute my worried brain. I know by worrying I am praying for the unwanted.

Enjoying the view, I engage in small talk. I could feel the desire to get the momentum of my thoughts moving forward as the car was moving forward down the highway.

As we arrived, I told the driver thank you and completed our transaction with a tip. Before I could get out of the car, I witnessed the driver rate me. Excuse me? It wasn't until this moment I realized this was a thing. I think I was slightly aware but never truly internalized it. Would living in awareness of being rated by an UBER driver actually change my behavior? He did give me a 5-star rating, but why? I then realized how subjective an entire rating system is. There are so many variables that come into play, for example, was the rating earned because I tipped, or was it self-serving for the driver, so he could quickly move on to the next driver? The old adage being, time is money, money is time. For whatever reason, I just ended a journey where I was off the topic of being rated. Encapsulating the idea that I need to go on a published author journey by staying true to the course, having gentle focus on my desired destination, filling my tank when I feel empty, showing appreciation for the ride, and staying off the topic of being rated.

This all seemed so profound yet so tidy. I knew there was more. I began to think of UBER's Community Guidelines. In order to access and effectively use the app, one must agree to safety measures and laws in order to maintain uber etiquette; there is a vast list of do's and don'ts. Bringing this idea to my own conscious awareness, I realized I am meant to set community guidelines for myself as I follow my inspired impulses. Reflecting on my own do's and don'ts, I choose to only focus on the do's. I love focusing on the wanted and not the unwanted.

As I think of my dos list, I tap into my higher self, she is a badass and I know she has boundaries. Here are my top three:

1. Do use your imagination to create your desired life.
2. Do enjoy the journey, allowing for self-care along the way.
3. Do give yourself a high rating and others will follow.

Number 3 spoke volumes to me. By giving myself low ratings, my vibration is impacted, and this could be mirrored to me in my physical reality. Are we hearing and receiving critical feedback, with some exceptions, that may be reflected through a vibration we are practicing concerning ourselves? Exploring areas where I am critical of myself, I self-soothe with knowing I am committed to my soul purpose alignment. When I am experiencing split energy, the moments of *I want it BUT*, I take the calibration to a better feeling state. I am reminded there is no assertion, only attraction. I contemplate what reviews I would love to attract, I allow visions of 5-star ratings to live at the forefront of my mind. I see myself reading comments that feel like satisfaction. This offers so much relief. Here is my major epiphany, my self-acceptance should not be CONDITIONAL on how others rate me. Rating myself from a place of unconditional love is all that matters. Do I for one moment think my inner being would rate me and comment about me from a place of negativity and criticism? The answer is a hard no. Allowing the love from my inner being offers delicious tingles from head to toe; absolute acceptance from source energy is all I need. I love knowing I am a powerful creator. I love knowing I only experience love and acceptance from my inner being, I love knowing I am already attracting readers who will appreciate my work, I love knowing that I heard my inner voice whisper to me to follow my passions, and I did.

Obviously, I also love appreciation rampages.

My journey is my journey. Like Uber, we are both committed to our own personal safety and arrival to our desired destinations. Whereas Uber has door-to-door standards, I have destination-to-destination guidelines. As our services evolve, we both evolve with updated features. I am driven by service and self-awareness, and when my manifestations are backed with pure intentions, then I know I am following my life's calling.

YOU CAN NOT ATTRACT FROM OTHERS WHAT YOU CAN NOT GIVE YOURSELF.

With this, I offer myself a 5-star rating and comment: THIS HAS BEEN ONE HELL OF A RIDE, BUT WORTH IT! I wouldn't change a damn thing! Most importantly, have fun.

1. Are you enjoying the journey towards your desires? Would you describe it as one of effort or one of ease? Effort creates more effort, ease creates more ease. What do you do daily to enjoy the journey? Elaborate.

2. Do possible criticisms from others hold you back from showing up in your life as your true desired self? If so, what inspired whispers in your ear are you ignoring? How can you empower yourself to listen? What does soul purpose alignment mean to you?

3. What are your personal community guidelines for yourself? With a focus on having personal boundaries, what are your dos for your life?

4. What type of environment and people make you feel safe? How can you have more fun following your desires?

5. Rate yourself and comment. Give yourself a 5-star rating and offer an appreciation rampage towards your excellence. Write from the perspective of your inner being and offer yourself praise from a place of unconditional love. Feel this at the visceral level.

Chew with your Mind Open

Attraction Point to Ponder 26

I can recall hearing the following quote by Robert Kiyosaki, "The size of your success is measured by the strength of your desire, the size of your dream, and how you handle disappointment along the way." With how my mind works, upon hearing and reading this quote, I fixate on the word, disappointment.

Recently I heard someone say they fear having friends because of the worry of being a disappointment. This resonated with me immediately. I found myself thinking about all of the social situations where I felt like I didn't belong. Life is an idea, and to me, friendships are an idea also. The idea or essence of friendships, through my perspective, lend themselves to being judged by others. The pandemic allowed me to become overly accustomed to not having a huge social calendar, and I also discovered that I love being alone. Emotionally, I believe I accept being alone more often than not, because it keeps me safe from the possibility of being socially critiqued. Intellectually, however, when I think about how we are social sapiens, one might say we need social interaction in order to truly thrive.

My son has been on a weight loss journey for the last two years, and we have had so many discussions around an individual's SET BODY WEIGHT (SBW). *Some research shows that our bodies have a natural weight or 'set point' that they will return to, regardless of what we eat and how much we exercise.* At this moment, I feel like I have a SET SOCIAL WEIGHT, where it does not matter how social I may attempt to be, regardless of what I do socially, my soul has a natural social weight in terms of how much I can commit to friendships. I default to wanting to be home more often than not. I consistently return to this point where I feel like I am not worthy of friendships because I may disappoint others, possibly with my presence, my discussion topics, and even my need to cancel last minute.

Full disclosure, I often leave coffee dates feeling depleted.

With all of this surfacing, I realize I am living extremely guarded. This explains why I saw myself wearing full knight's armor as I silenced my mind. The armor felt clanky, heavy and claustrophobic… I could barely breathe. This is not how I desire to live. However, I could feel my desire to be protected from head to toe.

My need to feel lighter was immediate, I then saw myself with a bullet-proof vest on. My thought was, at least my heart is protected, if not only just physically. There was room for silliness here, I began to lighten up, there was no way I would attend a social event wearing a bulletproof vest. I continued to think about my life in terms of feeling protected in a way that was socially acceptable to everyone watching. I then received an image of me in eighth grade getting ready for basketball practice. I wore wrist guards, knee brace, high tops, long socks and a mouth protector for my braces. I would present myself to my coaches, teammates and our cheering section feeling protected physically, knowing what I was wearing was appropriate. This felt a little better knowing I could dress for protection success, but again, this was only protection for my physical body, not my emotional state.

Sitting with the image of me playing basketball, I am realizing how insecure I was back then but I still showed up.

I am reminded of one of my favorite memories of my whole middle school basketball career... coming home and having a large bowl of cold cereal. I see myself opening the refrigerator, pulling a gallon of milk out and looking at the expiration date. Always so much appreciation for milk that was still good. I see myself putting the gallon of milk and the cereal box on the kitchen table and keeping both of them there as I eat my cereal.

I loved staring at the back of a cereal box and turning the box as I ate. I would read all of the information on the box, every last word. As I felt a true connection with my cereal box, and I am willing to admit that true friendship connections are something I crave just as much as those cereal moments. Reading a cereal box feels more authentic somehow than superficially staring at a smartphone. Within me exists the need for genuine connectedness in whatever form it shows up.

As I recall reading about any nutritional value of the cereal, I have always appreciated receiving the health benefits and balance with the food I eat. I expect the same from friends. Within my friendships, I want to feel healthy and balanced. Back then, the nutritional information was limited and probably not regulated but I remember thinking, my cereal is a strong source of iron and many vitamins. The words VITAMIN-FORTIFIED appear in my mind. My cereal moments were always my moments of total replenishment. Whether or not 2% milk and sugary cereal were good for my body does not matter, it is what I desired for my body at the time, and that is all that mattered.

Receiving the memory of the milk and cereal sitting on our kitchen table allowed me to tap into my cereal ritual in my life today. My 2% milk has been replaced with unsweetened almond milk and my sugary cereal box, now typically low-fat granola, is riddled with a plethora of nutritional value information according to serving size. Full transparency is what the current laws call for.

I desire full transparency in my relationships as well.

Slowly, I begin to realize that expiration dates can also be applied to friendships. This may sound harsh to some, but if something expires food-wise, we thoughtfully dispose of it. You would not drink spoiled milk and gut bomb your physical body, so why would we emotionally endure a friendship that was making us sick with stress and nausea? Friendships should be about replenishment, not depletion or even repulsion. Sometimes we have to get rid of friends in terms of moving on, because the relationship no longer serves us or possibly even them. There are people in my life who entered during a personal low vibe state of mind, and I know we were all meant to meet, but this does not mean we are meant to be. I have relationships that have "gone bad" over time. Like spoiled milk being removed from the fridge, I can apply the same expectations for spoiled relationships. I have boundaries for what I put into my physical body and this is a permission slip to do the same for my emotional body from a place of appreciation for all. The Food and Drug Administration has standards for food, and we have to have our own standards for our friendships.

As I see myself continue to stare at the milk and cereal on my life's table, I still think about nutritional value. We often read cereal boxes before we buy them, and tend to ask ourselves if this food product is nutritional. Sometimes we read about the possible harm of the ingredients, and we put the cereal box back on the shelf. Sometimes we read about the possible harm of the ingredients, and we still put it in our cart. We get to choose. This applies to friendships. We enter some relationships ignoring the ingredients which may harm our mental health, or we enter them hoping we will feel better despite the ingredients, which is conditional.

One major epiphany through this meditative journey is how I have evolved and changed concerning what I put into my grocery cart. Our food choices and needs evolve as we evolve. Similarly, our choices in friends and personal needs evolve as we evolve.

For example, growing up, I loved sleepovers, playing team sports, going to school, going to the mall with friends. I had a fear of missing out before I even knew FOMO was a thing. Now I live with the fear of being invited, FOBI. At this moment, my desire to be alone is high, but I want this state to only be in moderation and not extreme.

This all led me to think about nutrition values and portion control. I have always loved giving my physical body whatever it needs. I love feeling physically replenished, rejuvenated, and refreshed. What I don't like is to feel overly full, so I know my own portion control and there are some ingredients that are a hard pass. I do not measure my food out ever, I simply know when I am full. When I am satiated, I stop eating.

I am now realizing that the fear of disappointing others does not need to be my main ingredient, nor does social isolation. I can apply the idea of portion control. I can pour into others and allow others to pour into me at a serving size that feels good. This means being deliberate and intentional with my needs and being open to others offering the same to me. When we pour a bowl of cereal and milk, we know just the amount and we stop before the bowl overflows. I desire friendships, but I desire to be deliberate and intentional with how much is too much. I can remember my mom asking, "What are you going to have to eat?" Sometimes I would reply, "I am not hungry." She would try to coax me to eat anyway. For my friendships, I desire to say aloud, I am full, I have no room to be social today, and they honor that. No coercion. If I do show up, they understand my need for portion control so I can leave when I have had enough. The introverts of the world will understand this.

My setting boundaries also applies to the nutritional value of relationships. If my soul is not being nourished and the ingredients are harmful, I do not have to partake.

I know what my stomach needs to feel full, in return, I know what my soul needs to feel full.

My needs may also change daily. Like regulated nutritional information on a cereal box, I desire to experience full transparency of what is good for me and what is truly being offered.

I close out this moment by missing the simplicity behind the moments of reading the backs of cereal boxes. There is a strong desire within me to feel more present, to sit at the table with others, looking at one another and not our phones. I constantly think about the expectations I have for myself and realize now I can have expectations for the people in my life. I am not a control freak per se, but I am realizing for me to thrive in friendships, I need to be an emotional portion control freak. Some days I just want dry cereal, sometimes a spoon full or an entire bowl or even the whole damn box. I desire people who accept my social appetite on any given day, with no harm to none.

If a relationship is good for me, into my life's grocery cart it goes. When I decide to indulge in friendship, it is measured based on what is good for the both of us. The portions will vary from any given day…we can range from simply texting, to actually talking on the phone, to actually meeting in person. I measure with my heart, always, and my true friends will sit at life's table with me as we mutually meet each other where we are on that day. No judgment, no feelings of disappointment, just being present in the given moment and our distractions are non-present as we get back to the basics of life. The people in my life deserve the same focus I gave those cereal boxes, and so do I.

I close this meditation by being reminded of a saying I heard growing up, "Everything tastes better when you share it with friends." I now know, everything tastes better when you are in a state of appreciation for being true to yourself, alone or with company.

My highest desire is for my life to be delicious in every way. Soulful satiation holds the highest nutrient value for me, and I am the one pushing and filling my cart with emotions, thoughts, and feelings that nourish me.

I close with this friendly reminder: *When you speak your needs, don't speak with your mouth full, speak with your heart full and an open mind. Finally, we can all only hear someone else slurping their cereal for so long, and that includes ourselves before we do something about it. We all have our limits. Give yourself grace and have boundaries with others.*

1. Think of a time you felt completely protected, offer details. How can you allow for the feeling of being protected to occur more often? Do you have an inanimate object that offers protection, do you take it in public with you to feel secure?

2. Do you think about the nutritional value of what you put into your physical body? Yes or no, elaborate. Explain how you might increase the nutritional value of what you put into your emotional and physical body from a place of self-love.

3. Do you have relationships in your life that make you feel depleted? Are any of them way past their expiration date? Choose one person or circumstance causing you stress and possible nausea. Are you open to releasing them from your life, or at least putting them in the back of your mental fridge? Explain.

4. What do you desire from a friendship? What do you offer to a friendship? Place a focus on reciprocation and balance. Set an intention with your desired friendship by writing down what would be the ideal ingredients in a friendship that satiates your soul.

5. How are you willing to be deliberate and intentional with your own emotional portion control? How much is too much? Give examples of how you can set boundaries for yourself as a friend to others, knowing you can be the one who pushes the cart and controls what you put in it.

Here Comes Trouble

Attraction Point to Ponder 27

In my adult years, I asked my loving dad why he would discipline me as a young child. His answer was unsettling to the both of us in so many ways, he responded with deep regret in his voice, "I wanted you to be perfect." My dad admitted he foolishly thought that if my behavior was in check, people would think home life was in check as well. Having a childhood where there was divorce, alcoholism, poverty, and overall adversity, the very young version of me took on the very big job of distracting others from my family's real issues. How? By striving to be perfect. In hindsight, my now very present dad knows this was fear-based parenting, and I was being manipulated to be the red herring deflecting from the imperfect seas I called home.

One particular memory comes to mind, it took place on a Monday after my dad had organized a large bookshelf on his day off. I loved walking by his completed project, my love for books was amplified every time with each passing. On this particular Monday, I thought I would literally show-case my love for books by leaving out the ones that I had read that day. I made a nice pile on the floor near the bookshelf. My young mind's assumption based itself on the idea that my parents would be so proud of me because I used my time wisely by reading. I could not have been more off base with what was about to transpire. After a long day at work as a delivery man, my dad opened my bedroom door and asked, "Why are there books on the floor?" I innocently and excitedly told him that every book on the floor was the book I had read that day. He told me to go pick a book and that would be the first book I would use to begin putting the books back where they belong. As I cried, I felt guilt and embarrassment. What I thought was going to be a moment of shared excitement turned into a moment of shared shame. I felt the shame then, and my dad would feel the shame later as we looked back on this memory.

Fast forward many years later, as a latchkey child, now living with a single working mom, during my parents' divorce era, I felt responsible for watching other home alone children in our neighborhood. On one terrible day, a neighbor boy was being unruly, so I got really upset with him because I felt responsible for maintaining order with the disorder of having no adults around. When his mom came home, I shared with her how I handled the matter, and she came undone. The irony of this moment is I naturally emulated his mom's handling of misbehaviors. His mom's hot temper led me to go straight back to my house and to my room as I still had my roller skates on because I was hoping to go play after I reported what happened. With crocodile tears in my eyes, I can still picture myself getting into my bed crying because I was just emotionally berated by his mom. Once again, I thought I had done the right thing, for it only to be deemed the wrong thing and punishable. To this day, I can still feel the heaviness of the roller skates on my feet and the heaviness in my heart felt in that disastrous moment.

Memories with this theme of thinking I made the correct choice when I actually didn't through the eyes of others could fill an entire scrapbook.

I have learned to live with only briefly inflated excitement for doing the right thing, only to expect to be later deflated by getting into trouble for wrongdoings.

Intellectually, I believe the adult responses around me as a child were symptomatic of the emotional climate of the times we were living in. Nevertheless, the weathering effects of my childhood storms continue to erode away my excited thoughts on the daily. To this day, I always feel like if I bring the rainbow, I still am to be blamed for the rain.

Living in fear of coloring outside of the lines is exhausting, you have to live to be prepared, or your behavior could be wrongfully repaired with a punishment. I have lived preparing myself in so many ways, like always thinking about what I was going to say, how I was going to behave, what I was going to wear so my external choices would not reflect my home life's internal shit show. This is a trained behavior I brought into my adult life. I can go to the grocery store and still fear I will forget something and disappoint my family. I can plan a trip and fear everyone will be mad at me if the plans don't transpire accordingly. I can go to work and seriously walk through the door wondering who I will manage to disappoint that day, and even with a girl's night out, I worry I will say something wrong and ruffle feathers. In my marriage, I would wonder what my husband, no fault of his own, would come home mad about concerning something I did wrong despite all I did for my family. Now, to top it off, as my two children are now basically adulting, despite all of the love I offer them, I worry I will be in trouble with them because of something I did or do wrong as their mom.

My fear of getting into trouble is overwhelming, I feel the ick of it all, and I desire to be free from not only the ick but also the ache.

Relaxing my mind, I immediately see two swans coming together and making a heart.

I can recall learning how a reunited swan couple form the shape of a heart with their heads after being separated for weeks. This coming together of the two swans highlights the strength of emotions the birds have for one another.

When I think of most given situations, however, I feel overwhelmed with being in trouble and I see the heads involved being the clashing of the titans, not the shape of a heart.

I began to further think about what shape I bring to tête-à-tête, head-to-head conversations. Even though face-to-face conversations are often meant to be private, because of trust issues, they immediately feel public to me. My shape is not the other half of a heart, it is fucking warped, there is no shape, it's tattered and weathered from misuse. In this big puzzle of life, I feel like everyone's shape has maintained itself well over time, and I am the piece that is worn out. This makes me feel fucking dead inside, I have completely worn myself out thinking at any given moment I may be in trouble. My puzzle piece is tattered.

Did I want every hard conversation to be one of total love? Not necessarily.

Did I want to be a perfect puzzle piece? No, believe it or not, I do find beauty in my flaws.

Do I feel like all the puzzle pieces of my life, meaning people, will be mad at me if I don't accurately complete the coming together of thoughts by exactly fitting in? YES!

What shape would feel better than thinking I am the one that will mess up the whole coming together of everything? Every encounter, every conversation, when I say everything, I mean everything.

The immediate shape I received was a folded fan called an Ogi. The Ogi originated in Japan and is made of wooden or bamboo strips threaded together and secured by a rivet or pivot.

Never ever have I seen the shape of a puzzle piece outline like a folding fan, but this is what came up.

I imagined the fan cooling my face off. Once again, I feel like a hot mess. The fan cools me off physically, but I know I desire more for my heated emotional state.

This fear of being in trouble is a deep-rooted way of being for me.

With total clarity, I know in life, I don't want to be a folded fan. I want to be able to open myself up and be fully represented, but I also want to honor my comfort level with how much I am willing to open up about. My highest desire is to show up easily and readily with essentially a flick of the wrist or attention paid towards how much I am willing to show. A folded fan opens in a snap, there is no overthinking, it happens very leisurely, and when opened, the beauty is seen. A partially opened fan can be equally as beautiful but gives me time to prepare and be thoughtful. With a fan, no matter what I decide to do with it, I feel like I can't get it wrong…my life is in my hands.

I accept this. I desire to be more open, to stop overthinking, and to show the world all of my beauty, whether partially or completely. Again, I hold so much power in my own hands and thoughts.

I continue to think of the word fan and move it away from figuratively speaking to thinking of an actual fan in our life's arena. No fan of mine is going to yell out, "YOU ARE IN TROUBLE!!! YOU ARE SO BUSTED!! YOU ARE GOING DOWN!"

My true fans offer support.

My true fan is me.

I think of the things I could be feeling and saying to myself. "All is well," or "Everything is always working out." What I think is the best possible outcome may even be better than I could have ever imagined. The better it gets, the better it gets, as Abraham Hicks shares.

I begin to imagine a life where my life is not the shouts of being in trouble from the peanut gallery, but cheers from my own pep squad within.

As I release the thoughts of always being in trouble, I think of a life where I could have taken the time to truly pump myself up before a game, meeting, conversation, etc. I could have had more pep talks, more self-rallys, more self-team moments, and even more prayer.

Like a fan flapping air to my face, I could not only be more selective in how I am supporting myself, I could allow myself to feel and be refreshed by my own words and thoughts.

In a world where there is so much emphasis on target audiences, niches, and followers, it is at this moment I realize the true fan base I need to grow is in me, not outside of me.

I need to become my own ideal fan in order to attract supporters around me. When I allow thoughts about myself to be unsupportive, I am giving permission to others not to support me.

I also can call a timeout for myself, if I am whelmed over, I will not play overwhelmed. I can call a break before any conversation. I commit to speaking from alignment and never from being out of alignment.

The foundation of my personal fanbase is alignment.

I close out, thinking of what sign I would have posted above my life's locker room door to tap as I head out into the world. In the television show, Ted Lasso, Coach Lasso hangs a sign that reads "BELIEVE" above his office to motivate his team. Coach Lasso's sign inspires me to display an imaginary one that reads "RECEIVE". I see myself looking up and touching my sign. This idea of receiving is directed to myself, I am ready to hear my own cheering section that supports me with faith over fear. The louder my inner fanbase is heard and received, the quieter my inner critic becomes. Washing out the noise of my inner critic through receiving supportive words for me and from me also shuts down my receptivity to the idea of being in trouble. This is a huge win for me.

1. If you feel like you are going to constantly be in trouble, what life experience or experiences does this come from? You are still here, so explore the resiliency you have attained by continuing on despite what you have endured.
2. Why do you fold yourself together, appear closed off for some people? What conditions do you have in order to open up and be fully represented?
3. What is your *one word*? What word empowers you? How do you allow this word to not only be seen and heard, but to also be felt?
4. What sayings could you offer to yourself as if you are your ultimate fan base?
5. What is something you can do to easily cool off in a heated situation? When you are overwhelmed, how can you call your own time out in the game of life? This moment should be similar to how many describe meditation as nothingness, where and what can you do to experience nothingness? Remember, doing nothing is doing something.

Mind your own SPIRITUAL business

Attraction Point to Ponder 28

Just yesterday, I was listening to a conversation around anxiety. I have struggled with this recurring emotional response my entire life. I can recall navigating the pandemic, my son leaving for college, a recent move, a career change and so much more without feeling heightened, which seemed unusual. I actually convinced myself that I had my anxiety under control. I have been proud of myself up until this point, but after recently discussing anxiety, I realized I have only normalized my symptoms by infusing them into everything I call life. It had become such a way of life to me that I thought I overcame anxiety when actually I made my disrupted neurological state my norm.

My anxiety shows up with a sense of nervousness, an inability to relax, the world feels like it is unfolding rapidly and then completely slowly, my breathing is often dysregulated and I am overcome with some sense of impending danger. I believe that anxiety shows up differently for different people, maybe in the form of panic attacks, phobias, social anxiety, OCD and PTSD. Nevertheless, the struggle is real, very real.

Even as a little girl, I can remember my cheeks being red and feeling so flushed when faced with uncertainty. As a teenager, I actually pulled over my car once to control my breathing and regain full eyesight during an anxiety attack. And as an adult, when I worry, I have literally put both hands on the kitchen countertop to stay standing.

I thought I had come so far.

Ironically, however, my recent discussion about anxiety actually triggered my anxiety. Whereas I thought I had it under control, I am realizing it still has control of me. I still had all my moments, some call them episodes, I just excused them more easily now.

As one who has lived through so much uncertainty, I believe in the power of having certainty.

When I first quieted my mind, the image I received was an erupting volcano, and I recalled how Mt. St. Helens blew in Washington when I was in the third grade. Every time I have ever blown, or felt blown, I have always recovered, thankfully to some degree. Even now, when I think of the volcanic eruption that scared me as a little girl, the mountain has now rested for over forty years and has amazing evidence of recovery.

Loud and clear I then heard the word DORMANT.

Volcanoes are described as *dormant* when they stay cool for a long time without spewing hot lava and ash. Mount St. Helens has been dormant now since 1982. Like my anxiety, the volcano still has the ability to come to life, but the inactive state is one I appreciate. *Dormant* comes from the French *dormir,* "to sleep," and it refers to living things that are on a break. I appreciate the idea of simply being on a break or asleep as opposed to being completely dead inside. Being dormant is being temporarily at rest, and what I desire is to have my restful state to remain regulated for longer periods of time. I live knowing that at any given moment, my anxiety can become active, not only erupting but taking out everything in my path.

I felt a stronger desire to ease this a bit, the idea of spewing my uncontrolled emotions at any given moment was unsettling.

I then see a version of me packing for a trip frantically. Racing to the airport by car frantically. Running through the airport frantically.

All these frantic moments followed up with seeing a version of me finally relaxing on the plane.

I realize I don't have to have frantic moments in order to feel relaxed, and I don't have to allow my relaxed moments to turn into frantic ones.

I allowed myself to chill here in this moment, that moment where you have made the flight, you are finally seated, prepared for takeoff, and your body can let down.

I begin to think about the clothes I packed, and then begin to think of getting dressed in general. More often than not, I simply dress for physical comfort but I do care about my physical appearance.

Intuitively, I now feel a very strong desire to have my insides match my outsides.

Any time I experience success, I often ask myself, "Who am I to have this?" This statement alone feels like self-sabotage in the making.

So sometimes, when getting dressed, I think, why try to look good if I don't even feel good, and that turns into why desire good when I will just sabotage the good.

I then have this memory of my mom driving me to high school and her hot coffee spilled all over my outfit, and she insisted we turn around and go home so I could change. I told her no. With spilled coffee all over me, I was finally open to showing the world how I was really feeling… a stained mess outside and in. I was tired of acting happy when I wasn't. Over it.

When I then think of my insides matching my outsides, I am talking about being in such alignment in my inner world that the outer world feels and sees it. I don't want to feel like a stained mess inside, I want my personal vibration to be clean and ready for even better.

Here is where I recognize my personal growth. Although anxiety may control me in so many ways, I now make alignment a priority. Tending to my alignment as part of my morning routine allows me to get momentum going in the right direction before my day really begins.

I begin to let go of the idea that I have normalized my anxiety. It is still there, but not as crippling.

As I desire to be of service to others, I internalize that I must first be of service to myself.

When I think of service, I think of how I can impact the world by being a spiritual entrepreneur and by uplifting others. What I know is this, being of service means being connected to my inner world daily. For me, this is through meditation...no one knows me better than my inner being. My daily inner world journey is my intimate touchstone that grounds me in a place that is true to who I really am.

Alignment is where my life flows with ease, joy and flow.

For so many years, I lived out of alignment, life felt like effort, I bought into the hustle and the grind. I no longer desire to be of service from DOING, but from BEING.

Now, if coffee were to spill on my outfit, I would change. By making my alignment a priority, the stained mess no longer represents what is going on inside of me, and if it does, it is something I am willing to clean up.

I go back to my older self, and in appreciation I thank her for keeping me alive when I could not have been more out of alignment. I picture my older self thanking my higher self for choosing a lighter path. Their roles hold equal value and are seamless and beautiful.

I now go back to the idea of who I am to have such success...and shift to how I can be of service. But now I can feel how the idea of service is completely activated from a state of being connected and in alignment. Alignment is where I have clarity, feelings of calm, and I am content.

The Divine Download: BE OF SERVICE FROM A PLACE OF ALIGNMENT.

As I close this meditation, I am reminded of the song title from ANNIE, *You're Never Fully Dressed Without A Smile*. A smile is one thing, but having your smile supported through centered thoughts, emotions and feelings is how we effortlessly move through this world and our desires. Getting dressed, with our insides matching our outsides, means embodying our true selves.

215

1. How does anxiety show up in your body? What are the moments where you are entirely chilled out? How does being chilled out feel in your body?
2. Where do you find the courage to let go of uncertainty? What offers you feelings of total certainty? What allows you to feel like you can find your way through life's eruptions with total clarity?
3. Before you can be of service to others, explore first how you can be of total service to yourself.
4. How do you describe being in alignment? For you, what does it look like and feel like?
5. Recall a time you knew you were in total alignment, how can you allow that version of you to be more readily available in terms of service to others and yourself?

The Name Game

Attraction Point to Ponder 29

My birth name is Elizabeth, like the Queen of England herself. I have watched so many video clippings where the Queen hears her name and accepts it with grace, she wears her name proudly like the royal crown itself.

Even as I see Elizabeth on this very screen, I realize how foreign my own first name has become to me. As I was growing up, I went by Liz, Lizza, Lizzy and even Beth. Unwelcomed use of my first name during my childhood happened when I was in trouble with a capital T. If my mom or dad referred to me by my full first name, I knew I had done something upsetting. Sadly, yet, thankfully, I have lived in appreciation that I was blessed with a first name that I could modify, because I had developed an aversion to hearing my full name. Now, as an adult, I feel inspired to let all the powers of association concerning being called Elizabeth to be set free. This was recently activated in me as I watched Queen Elizabeth celebrate her 70th year as the ruling monarchy in England. She is not Queen Liz, Queen Lizza, Queen Lizzy, Queen Beth, she is Queen Elizabeth, and I desire to be the ruling leader of my reality free of the mishandling of my name. An individual's real first name is worthy of being crowned with rich meaning, not poor memories. There is sadness here, some feelings of helplessness, and anger for how my name was misused not only by it being used to signify I was in trouble, but also with a tone that I found to be frightening as a little girl.

Essentially, growing up in my childhood home and being called Elizabeth felt very punitive.

In elementary school, friends saying Elizabeth when referring to me felt like name calling. I dreaded substitutes because I knew they would roll call using my first name.

In high school, when my full name was announced on the intercom to come to the office, it was the longest walk of shame. I assumed I was about to be suspended, even if no wrongdoings had occurred.

In college I read the book, WHEN AN OWL CALLS YOUR NAME. This book's main character, Mark, is returning from scattering the ashes of a Kwakiutl friend, and he hears an owl call his name. In Kwakiutl lore, if an owl calls your name, it means you are about to die. Of course, I envisioned the owl calling my name, the name the owl would use is undeniably *Elizabeth*.

In the workplace, if someone called me by my full first name, I would feel it in my core, my inner child would become frightened, and I assumed I was going to be reprimanded.

When I saw my full name on my marriage certificate, I was mortified not only to see my first name but to also see it next to my new marital last name.

Intellectually, I realize that the human behavior experts of the world may validate my defensive response because my whole being experienced the negative connotations of Elizabeth during my most formative years, but I know I would also be encouraged to free myself of this mental mess.

In full hindsight, even with total strangers, when most people called me Elizabeth, I have always felt they wanted my full attention in a negative manner.

Now I desire to give myself full attention in a positive manner, Elizabeth is my first name, and the hostage takeover I feel with its use needs to be put to rest. I seriously feel like my own mental terrorist at times.

With all this within me, I close my eyes and see a very old-fashioned typewriter. I think of the scene from the movie ATONEMENT, remembering seeing this movie title being typed out as part of many scenes. Like the meaning of atonement, I desired repair and satisfaction with my own name. I have lived offended and emotionally injured by the misuse of my first name, and I could feel the need for reconciliation. I begin to think of how my name looks typed out, then I see Elizabeth represented in cursive writing, then a rubber stamp version of my signature, and finally my name on print paper using a pencil. So often, I can choose how my name is presented in visual form. What I wanted to control however is how it is presented audibly.

My mind is reminded of the saying, "If no one is in the forest when a tree falls, does it still make a noise?" I am reminded of how a friend of mine will ask the deep and hysterical question of, "If my wife is in the forest alone, and something goes wrong, is it still my fault even though I am not there with her?" He would always jokingly reply with a yes.

The great question of the trees allows me to be reminded that sound is vibration, and we are the translators of sound. If no one is there to translate the sound, then I find confidence knowing there is no sound when trees fall.

I am a translator of sound. I apply meaning to the sounds I hear.

This reminder feels empowering.

If trees were falling around me, I would assure my physical safety while covering my ears. I may even choose to drown out the sound of the trees with my own voice. My goal would be to protect myself at all levels.

I think of the meanings I have attached to hearing Elizabeth: its use is often loud, it's offensive, it's violating and degrading. Now I must ask myself if I have attempted to protect myself at all levels, whereas my friend would say yes, he is in the wrong whether he is in the forest or not,

I am saying no to having ever protected myself from audio harm. I have never plugged my ears, I have never fled to safety, and I have never attempted to drown out someone else's words by offering boundaries. I have never spoken up for myself and shared how I find its misuse to be offensive.

My boundaries would be to simply state, "Please do not use my name in that manner." This is what I desire. No justification offered. Just being pleased that I openly stated what I want without justification. This is my fucking birth name. I don't need my crown straightened by others, I need to straighten my own crown by using my empowered voice.

As feelings of standing in my steady pour in, straightened crown and all, I am realizing that the use of Elizabeth towards me can depend on the context of the discussion, or who the person delivering the name is. I think of my relatives, my friends, teachers, bosses, and I am ready to accept the fact that I am a translator of sound vibration. Taking ownership of my vibration translations is part of my journey. I am becoming very aware that I give what I hear and how I hear it the internalized meaning. Accepting the fact that I can either tune out those that are offensive, or I can speak up for myself, or I can translate what is being said as my higher self, no matter what, I am the keeper of my own forest.

I can give myself and others the grace I desire.

As I close out this meditation, I realize I have never taken the time to look up the meaning of Elizabeth. I have lived so consumed by the delivery of my name, I never hit the pause button to learn the actual meaning of my name. Immediately deciding to do so, it reads: God is my oath; The name Elizabeth has religious roots and origins in Hebrew. Elizabeth can have several meanings, including "My God is an oath", "My God is abundance", and "pledged to God".

What is an oath I have for myself? I can offer boundaries concerning my first name's use when necessary.

What is the abundance in this reframing of how I hear my name? The bounty exists knowing all sounds are vibrations, I am the translator of sound, I interpret the meaning of the tones and choose to experience meaning towards my higher purpose.

What do I pledge to myself? My personal pledge is to give meaningful and thoughtful context to any circumstance where my first name is being used.

Every time someone says Elizabeth, they are saying, "God is my oath," no matter how the word is spoken or in what tone, this is what is being proclaimed. The loyal promise I now offer God, the Universe, myself, and others is seeing my name as a blessing. May my faith in myself and a higher power be what I hear and feel when anyone calls my full name in its entirety, this is my new benediction. Throughout my entire existence, I would rather live with a lifelong agreement to celebrate my name as I choose to hear it spiritually. Living triggered by my first name now feels so counterintuitive. The definition of Elizabeth is powerful, and the meaning I personally give to the word's resonance holds even more power.

It is with full acceptance I realize we are all not only selective listeners, but we are also selective translators. I came into this meditation thinking that, by default, we can simply selectively hear what we want to hear. I leave this meditation leveling up, knowing we can translate what we hear with meanings not only for our own higher good but for that of others. As spiritual and social beings, we are all listeners and translators of sounds, meanings, and vibrations.

My reality suddenly feels like royalty, and hearing my name with grace will be one of my crowning achievements. Let the trees fall around me, I am ready. I am steady.

1. What does your full first name mean to you? When people use your full first name, how does it feel? What variables come into play, like circumstances, family, etc.?
2. Are you the keeper of your own forest? When you hear things that make you feel unsafe or unprotected, do you offer personal boundaries? Elaborate.
3. Are you open to accepting that you can translate any words or tones to serve your higher good? Give an example of a circumstance your higher self may have interpreted differently to better serve you in personal expansion.
4. What are some personal oaths and commitments you can offer to yourself in your pursuit of happiness?
5. Identify some areas in your life where you can offer yourself more grace. Knowing you don't have to rely on others to straighten your own crown, what can you do for yourself to feel more balanced and composed?

Flare Ups

Attraction Point to Ponder 30

This last year, I decided to take the year off from work in education... pandemic, turning fifty, my daughter's senior year in high school and relocating back to my hometown. Too much is too much. Full disclosure, with everything going on last year, I felt like I hit rock bottom. Feeling dead inside, I felt like I had nothing left. NOTHING. I have worked since I was very young, I was beyond tired. Yet this was a year where I needed to show up for me and my family, and I knew I could not give my job 100%. I could not work with elementary students who were in a trauma tornado when I was having my own natural disaster. Not even having the energy to make drinking water a priority, I knew I was in an emotional and physical drought. I knew I needed to quit my job, so I did.

When one actually desires to lay flat on a rock bottom surface until fully recovered, sprawling out and finally getting rest, it is time to stop accelerating and start braking. I needed a fucking break by putting on the brakes.

Yes, I said it, rock bottom was a desired state.

Tragically yet thankfully, my rock bottom felt like solid ground. I could rest, reset, and start over.

Knowing everyone's rock bottom happens for different reasons, it is very personal, I own mine happening because I was over life feeling hard. As I think about this, I never again want my rock bottom to not happen so abruptly, and if this feeling ever happens again, I want my bottom to be where the rock part is my personal strength in my life's rubble.

I begin to think about how we always hear people reference others as their rock, the person who offers solid support. Thankfully, I still desired to be that for myself and my loved ones but from a place of self-care first.

In this moment of reflection, I recall phrases directed towards me like, you are rock solid, you are my rock, and you are solid as a rock. I always had uplifting rock phrases directed towards me in my life. But as I hit the pause button on my life by quitting my career, I did not anticipate the rock throwing in terms of judgment from others. Now the phrases are, I can't believe you quit, what are you thinking, when are you going to figure this out, what happened to you… so much verbal rock throwing. I was being stoned to death and enough was enough. The irony of it all was too much. I was once judged for having been a working mom with young children, and now being judged for staying home with my daughter for her last year in high school.

Through it all, I remained appreciative of desiring to recover and rejuvenate, I knew I would eventually get back up, as opposed to doing the unthinkable.

With a pit in my stomach, I quiet my mind and am offered a memory of our family's boat that happened many years ago during my adult years. The three of us in our life jackets: my mom, her husband and I watched the sunset in the middle of the Puget Sound, and the moment was glorious, and nightfall came quickly afterwards. Without any current desire to go into the mechanics of it all, when we went to start the boat, the anti-freeze tank blew, we took cover, and the boat lost all power. Here we were in the middle of vast water, and it was pitch dark aside from the slight light of the moon. My family recalled being given a single flare when they first bought the boat. As there were no other boats around us, we were given one opportunity to seek help. Knowing hope floats high, my mom raised the flare and shot it, and we waited and waited with hope. There, in the near distance, was a large boat with a light on approaching us. They immediately offered to tow us in. So much thankfulness at this moment. So much appreciation.

This memory gave me a reminder that I have always had a reserve of flares within me. I still knew I could ask for help, and it would show up. I have always eventually shot flares high up in the sky when I was alone in my darkest hours, and thankfully, with the help of others, I was brought back to shore. I am still here. When I wanted to drown, I treaded and kept swimming. When I wanted to be lost, I was found. When I wanted my boat to capsize, I stayed afloat. Again, I am still here.

Then comes another memory of playing THE BOAT GAME during physical education in elementary school. My gym teacher, Mrs. B, had labeled the four walls of the gym with signs that read: Bow: Front of a boat. Stern: Rear of a boat. Starboard: Right side of a boat. Port: Left side of a boat. Mrs. B would call out a part of the boat and we would run to the announced labeled wall, the last couple students to arrive would have to sit out, and we would play until there was only one survivor. I would always run with all of my might, and my teacher would praise my competitive spirit. Looking back, I did not participate from a place of competition. Even at a young age, I was driven by the need to completely exhaust my anxiety so I didn't completely go overboard, and I wanted to be a survivor and not a victim. To this day, I walk five miles daily, not for the physical benefits, but to allow the brisk bilateral movement to ease my anxious thoughts.

Sadly, I then think about my gym teacher asking us to line up in single file order. I wanted her to know that I never wanted to be the line leader or the caboose. I wanted to be in the middle of it all and experience order. I have a distinct memory of wishing she could call out the need for order to my family, and there would be everything lined up for me in a predictable and manageable manner. My young life's chaos desired order, and fast forward many years later, I still craved single file order. I wanted my life events to line up and follow along, no hitting, no screaming, no touching, no running, and no cutting in front of others. A life where personal space is honored and everyone keeps their hands and thoughts to themselves. Indoor voices, please don't speak unless you have something nice to say.

I now continued to think of life on a boat, and I could see myself relaxed reading a book… I knew at this moment my body was beginning to finally calm down. Laid out on the deck, I felt my body rocking along on an anchored boat with light waves underneath. Feeling the book in my hand, I love knowing this book was self-selected. All of my current adult reading selections are chosen by me. So much of my life already had been round-robin moments where I would wait for my turn to read, or the reading was assigned to me, or was dictated by a college syllabus, or was recommended to me in order to save my marriage, or as part of a book club or for self-help purposes. I no longer have deadlines, assignments, or analysis expectations: "Be ready to discuss the assigned reading" bullshit. Where I am in my life now is building my own book library based on my own criteria and my own decision-making skills. I was no longer being academically graded, I was no longer having to talk about a book I didn't enjoy reading, and my self-help books were recommended to me by me.

Reading is now for pure pleasure and personal growth, as life should be. I turn the pages, I read as fast and as slow as I want, and I jump ahead and skip the boring parts should I choose to do so. I HOLD MY LIFE'S BOOK. I am the author. I am the publisher. I am the main character, the theme, the setting, and the plot.

My life can be a total page turner, or it is a slow read. It is up to me.

The characters around me are irrelevant and so are their opinions. I am on my own journey as narrated by my thoughts, emotions, and feelings. I close this time, knowing if others want to rock my boat, throw stones, or outrun me… it's fine. I am solid. I also embrace the idea that someone else does not have to call out a single file order to my life in order to have it happen. I have routines and procedures that I can put into place to assure my safety while releasing the chaos. Anyone is welcome into my life, as long as they can behave in a manner that doesn't rock my boat because I am the captain of my own ship. I AM THE CAPTAIN. Clinging to the feeling of my favorite book, my flares, and my life jacket, I reopen my eyes, knowing I have always floated up from rock bottom, I have always come up for air, and I always will.

A new truth for myself is remembering I always have flares ready to signal for help, the people in my life can no longer rock my boat by being judgmental, and my desire for order is knowing I can be towed to safer shores from a place of love and acceptance.

In terms of hope, I now recall the beautiful quote from the actual movie HOPE FLOATS, when Birdee Pruitt says,"Childhood is what you spend the rest of your life trying to overcome. That's what momma always says. She says that beginnings are scary, endings are usually sad, but it's the middle that counts the most. Try to remember that when you find yourself at a new beginning."

I trust myself and that is all that matters. I am safe. I have hope. Knowing I will never jump overboard, I simply rest, knowing eventually I will be ok with my beginning, middle and end… eventually.

1. Knowing one's own rock bottom is personal, what does it look and feel like for you? Are you open to seeing rock bottom as an opportunity to rest, reset and get back up?
2. For your lowest moments, what do you have in reserve that prevents you from completely going overboard or drowning? What are your ultimate coping mechanisms? How do you signal for help?
3. Who are the people in your life throwing stones at you with judgment? Why do you give these characters so much relevance, how can you rewrite the role they play in your life?
4. In your anxious moments, what do you do to release your anxiety?
5. What gives your life a feeling of order?

Ain't No Mountain High Enough

Attraction Point to Ponder FINAL ROUND

Recently, I have had a situation that feels like I am being totally taken advantage of financially. Feeling taken advantage of is very crippling for me, and my highest desire is to release this. I no longer want to be a pushover, I no longer want to feel bulldozed, I no longer want to feel like an easy target.

I have memories of giving away my lunch money to bullies as a little girl, giving adults my babysitting money for her cigarettes, giving my college books away to people not wanting to pay the bookstore price so they can buy alcohol, and paying for others so they don't feel put out in social situations.

Being taken advantage of financially is so active within me and shows up in the form of severe headaches and a stomach ache, and I feel distracted from my present reality.

I close my eyes and see a sunset, and this allows me to take in the moment. As I absorb the vision of a sunset, I can feel my breathing begin to slow down, and my body begins to relax. As I look on I see the outline of a mountainscape, it all looks absolutely stunning. I hear the words, "It's the climb." That's how this situation feels, it feels like a climb. I am exhausted going through this uphill battle. I know that Source within me would not want to amplify these feelings, so I begin to think about the physical hills and mountains that I have hiked in my life. I have a love for hiking, and interestingly enough, I begin to realize that I have not hiked in a long time. One powerful component I love about deep state meditation is recalling activities and people, and moments that bring you joy. Hiking brings me total joy, I love being outdoors and getting exercise while taking in the scenery. I tap into this further. I think of the preparation I do prior to a hike. For example, I put on proper shoes, clothing, I eat a healthy breakfast, I pack nourishing snacks, I stretch, and I hydrate. Being prepared offers me feelings of readiness and safety.

I love my hikes and my walks, and when I am on them, I feel so good as I appreciate doing well for my mind, body, and soul.

And in comes my epiphanies. I am realizing that I place so much attention on prepping for physical activities, and I can allow myself to do the same for mental and emotional journeys.

This is what I hear loud and clear: If you take advantage of yourself, others will take advantage of you. If you don't take advantage of yourself, others will not take advantage of you.

Was I taking advantage of myself, and as a result, others were taking advantage of me? I have to own in this moment, that this has indeed been a theme in my life, and I admittedly feel as if I do take advantage of myself within my emotional climbs. I prepare for my daily journeys through meditation, journaling, and exercise, so part of me feels like I do. In a calm but confused state, I ask for clarity on how I can stop taking advantage of myself when I am being taken advantage of or, even better, to prevent others from doing so altogether.

I am given the vision of finishing a marathon. Finishing a marathon feels exhilarating and rewarding. I am then given a peaceful sight of me sitting at the top of a mountain after a long hike, as I look out at the view I feel so much gratification and appreciation. My desire to be more present in my life is stronger now more than ever.

Immediately I realize I can be more present by bringing the feelings I want to feel at the end of this situation into my present. My mind desires to feel better now, not later. Tapping into the outcome not from a place of being attached to an exact outcome, but the feeling the outcome would give me, brings the experience back to me. I am taking advantage of myself by attaching feelings that are negative to the situation, when I actually have the power to focus on my desired feelings. When I place the focus on myself and when I place the focus on the delicious feelings of enjoying and completing a climb, my journey will feel better. The Universe demonstrates an amazing presence around me while I am on a hike… I can channel my energy, making myself the center of the Universe during stressful situations. I don't hike feeling totally frustrated and stressed the entire time, I hike feeling primarily exhilarated.

Uphill climbs can even feel uplifting, if I allow them to.

I set an intention with this current financial situation by tapping into how I can use my mind to feel good now. The dominant emotion I desire is relief, so I begin to think how I can feel relief now. I know the Universe is my hiking partner, I know I am here for personal expansion, I know I love inspiring others, but I also am reminded to inspire myself. The ultimate inspiration I can offer others, including myself, is to feel good on the journey. I am reminded that I hold the map, I can take breaks when needed, I regulate my breathing, I can prepare, I can reroute, I can rest, I can take it all in, I can hydrate, I can celebrate the journey during my emotional, spiritual climbs before, during and after.

Beginning to think about it all, it is with high realization that I am in this current financial situation in an out of alignment state. I haven't felt good about it, so there is further momentum to events that don't feel good.

Tapping into feelings of relief further, I ask myself how I could have better prepared for this journey. Immediately, I was reminded to only take next steps after I have first tended to my personal alignment. I am reminded that a negative emotion may be experienced because my inner being is not in agreement with what is happening, so I can rest and wait until my emotional state is at ease.

During this journey, I can focus on my feelings by thinking about feelings of relief, like a tall glass of water on a hot summer day. I can allow those feelings now.

After this journey, I can sit at the top of life's mountain in a reflective state, taking in the scenery and offering appreciation for what I have experienced.

I am the center of the Universe, I am a powerful creator, I can feel good now, and life is a feeling journey, and I can always tap into my inner guidance system to know if I am on the right path or not.

I stretch before any hike… I now think of ways I can stretch when faced with mental and emotional challenges. The stretch may simply be setting an intention to not complicate things with my crazy-making intensity… relax and just be.

Before I close out this meditation, I once again sit with the sunset for a while. Again, I begin to think of my desire to hike more, to see more sunsets, to relax, to live in relief knowing all is well, and appreciate the journey.

By not taking advantage of myself, I also feel a heightened desire to better take advantage of the beauty all around me.

All of life's climbs, detours, and uphill experiences carry a backpack, and the emotions, feelings, and thoughts I put into my life's backpack have meanings determined by me. I desire for life to feel lighter and lighter by living in alignment with a focus on feeling good now, not later. I can also offer relief to any heaviness I feel within my emotional backpack by dealing with the things in life that are weighing me down. We are human bodies on a spiritual journey as we are spiritual beings having a human experience.

As I process all of this now, I think of some of the lyrics from my daughter's favorite song as a little girl "The Climb" by Miley Cyrus.

No, I am not breaking, I am making. I appreciate being reminded that I am creating my life with my head and emotions held high and enjoying the climbs. It is not about how fast I get there…it is about how I *feel* with every step I take. Life and manifestation is a feeling journey, and I am reminded that it feels good to feel good. Release resistance and allow from a place of total alignment.

1. How does anxiety physically show up in your body? What do you do to soothe discomforting physical states of being?

2. Are you open to the idea that a negative emotion is your inner guidance communicating with you that you are out of alignment? Have you ever ignored your intuition, you knew it wasn't for the best, but did it anyway? What was the outcome? When has your intuition served you?

3. How can you better prepare yourself for situations where the emotional backpack feels heavy?

4. After a perceived stressful situation, how can you allow yourself to reflect and appreciate the circumstance so you experience personal expansion? In a situation that is causing you stress, how can you provide evidence to the Universe that you have learned powerful lessons?

5. For all of us, allow this life to be a song where we individually give meaning to the lyrics. Embrace the idea that what we all hear has neutral meaning, we offer the meaning based on our own interpretations. Explore the meanings you are giving to situations that are causing you stress, how can you tap into better feelings and bring those higher feelings in now?

"What we perceive and what we understand depends on what we are."

— Aldous Huxle

Releasing Resistance With Clients

As a hypnotist, I feel very compelled to share some client stories to demonstrate how through spiritual guidance you too can receive beautiful messages that come from your inner being. These divine downloads are supported by unconditional love and infinite intelligence.

Breathe in and embody the gift of guidance as follows.

For my single mama who desired a new home for her and her children:

Fly in the face of opposing things others believe by giving up everything that is weighing you down... you have always had the wings, this was the theme of our conversation.

This is the powerful message she received:

I am settling for less with my current home but it is fueling my desire for more. I have the power of my own vibe, no one else does. It is all mine. Everything I desire is mine. It is already done. My manifestations are backed with pure intentions. I can walk into the new doors of my dream home with strong knowledge and a high sense of confidence. When I panic, I can self-soothe, pivot and find better feeling thoughts. Don't feel bad about where I live now, create from this space, build my dream home in my mind and soul from a place of excitement about what is to come and appreciate what is.

YOUR INNER SELF IS YOUR DREAM HOME, LIVE IN YOUR BEING NOW AS IF THE DREAM *HOUSE* ALREADY EXISTS.

Primary image: KEYS on a keychain

For my client who couldn't find a job that matched her desire:

One of my clients recently completed all of her academic aspirations and yet was "in her head" about being worthy enough to get a job.

The theme for this conversation was allowing, and here is what she downloaded:

When I see my own worth, others will too. By coming from a place of love for myself, I will manifest a workplace that loves me. I can be excited when others want to do things for me. (Her best friend wanted to drive her and she responded, "I don't want to be a burden." What an amazing way to understand personal feelings of self-worth. Someone was offering her something... and her vibration was that of being burdensome. That vibe would cross over to the workplace.) I can do anything, and if it works and if it doesn't and that is ok. I am always learning. I am always growing. It is ok to not know everything. I am worthy of having all of my desires. My inner being desires comfort, calm, feelings of safety, relief and happiness. When I am at peace, I feel like I am home with myself.

YOUR IDEAL CAREER WILL HAPPEN WHEN YOU SEE YOURSELF AS IDEAL.

Primary imagery: A cozy fireplace

For my client who regretted the financial decisions she made with an ex.

She wants to buy a house and she has so much anger towards herself because she made several poor financial decisions with her ex, which led to the loss of her home and her job. As we allowed for clarity, she was able to go back and relive the moment where she heard her inner guidance say, "Don't do it," when she met him and she did it anyway. With a permission slip to herself, she was able to go back in time and hear the words, "Don't do it," but this time from a place of total empowerment, she listened. Moving forward... She knows she will listen, truly listen to her inner voice and act accordingly. This was her stepping into her power. This was her remembering she is a BADASS, it was no longer <u>her ex's</u> voice she was hearing, it was her voice, and now going into buying a home for herself, independent of a partner, she now heard, *"I can do it," from within and that changed how she walked, talked, breathed, and stood. Keep saying, "I CAN DO IT," and feel it in your soul.*

THIS LIFE IS A FEELING JOURNEY.

Primary imagery: Can of fresh paint

For my client that desires to be famous...

As she was guided through her emotions around publicly performing, she imagined for a moment telling herself, "I am a person of the world," and feeling so much connectivity from others and to others. She realized as we put ourselves out there in the world of social media, we may face some criticism, and this is where we may feel the disconnect. She shifted to showing compassion for herself and others and stepping into her power with knowledge. She heard this:

Instead of allowing the critics to knock you out of your steady... stay in your steady, and you can be more present to perform.

If you face a disparaging comment through social media, your goal is to hold your steady.

When YOU EXIST IN THE NOW MOMENT, YOU ARE LOVE. Yes, it may FEEL alone, but there is an observable and unobservable Universe all around you.

You are the Universe, one who is shooting stars of harmony, forgiveness, and peace. You can laugh at comments instead of allowing them to make me feel inad-

equate. Tell your inner critic to shut the F&$ up. You are the galaxy and anyone is lucky to be in your orbit.*

YOUR INNER BEING HAS A LOUDER VOICE THAN YOUR INNER CRITIC.

Primary imagery: Planets among the entire galaxy

For my client who cheated on her boyfriend out of spite...

When she and her boyfriend got into a fight, she was so upset she went out and cheated on him. When completely connected, she was able to see herself to be entirely encapsulated by a golden egg and stated: My new story is one of self-love, I am independent, I am allowing feelings of independence in, I deserve love, I give myself the attention I deserve, I can high-five myself, ONLY PEOPLE WHO COME TO ME FROM LOVE AND ABOVE can enter my sacred container. I can reach for better feeling thoughts with constructive behavior vs. destructive behavior. Her beautiful imagery came from a place where she saw herself as THE GOLDEN EGG.

Remember the story Aesop told about the goose and the golden egg? The lessons are innumerable. The fable is about a poor farmer who one day discovered in the nest of his pet goose a glittering golden egg, and when he had it appraised, the egg was pure gold. The farmer couldn't believe his good fortune, and day after day, he awoke to rush to the nest and find another golden egg. With his increased wealth came increased greed and impatience. Instead of waiting for another day, the farmer decided to kill the goose so he could get them all in one day. But when he opened the goose, he found it empty. There were no golden eggs, he had no way of getting more.

Care for your own goose, don't destroy yourself with your own thoughts of impatience and greed, allow yourself to feel wealthy with self-love. Be patient with your own healing and know that self-love is the golden egg.

ALLOW FOR SACRED SPACE FOR YOUR HEALING.

Primary Image: A Golden Egg

For my client who was feeling incredibly sad:

As she described the happy version of herself, how she breathed, danced, talked, walked, dressed and where she felt happiness in her being, she realized how much she stepped away from happiness.

As she explored this, she realized that sadness and grief, it is a testimony to our capacity to love. We feel deeply because we love deeply.

For this client, she wanted to literally move away from her life from a place of urgency. We took a moment and we dropped the oars and allowed for her to tune into feelings of ease, calm, and peace. We asked her spirit guides to allow for the path of least resistance, and to not only move her physically along a path paved by peace but also to allow feelings of peace to flow through her. For all of us, when we vibe from PEACE, we will see more evidence of PEACE in our physical reality. It was during this visualization, she had a memory of dancing on a beach with these lyrics from Disney's POCAHONTAS, *Just Around the Riverbend:* What I love most about rivers is, you can't step in the same river twice, the water's always changing, always flowing…

She found peace knowing the waters are always changing, she is not stuck in sadness.

Drop the oars, chill out, OBSERVE, and allow the peaceful unfolding of the path the Universe already has you on.

ALLOW FOR EASE, JOY AND FLOW.

Primary Imagery: A river flowing downstream

For my client who desires to Fall in LOVE:

She is a real estate investor redefining her story… Her starting point was, "I NEED TO BE DOING SOMETHING", "I NEED TO GET BUSY", "I AM NOT WORKING HARD ENOUGH" in the area of love and business.

Know this, when we come from a place of struggle, we create more struggle. When we come from a place of effort, we create more effort. When she thought about her next purchases and her next relationship, our breakthrough came with the realization, *she is the investment.* Her vibrational setpoint was tuned into effort when she allowed for ease, this is the divine download we received:

BE so excited for what is next, imagine seeing your life as a book where you are hanging onto every page, YOU CANNOT WAIT for what is next, yet you are patient. Satisfaction and delight in your now moments feel good. We can peruse each moment, line by line, with giddy feelings of anticipation and ease. YOUR LIFE CAN BE AN ACTUAL PAGE-TURNER, your journey gets to be so good. Get cozy, and allow the unfolding of one's story. Follow your flow page by page.

YOU ARE THE MAIN CHARACTER.

Primary Imagery: A romance novel

For my client that was fed up with her weight loss journey:

Let's talk about weight loss. Our next journey begins with an individual who is doing all the things with total attachment to the outcome: counting calories, fitness routine, personal trainer, getting on the scale.

When she tuned in, here is what divine guidance offered. First and foremost: hope, renewal, and revival are her power words. Her inner desire to feel more of this was immediate. Her fixation with numbers on the scale was depleting all of this.

Our download continued with these beautiful nuggets: Your inner being desires admiration and adoration without conditions. EXIST WITHOUT THINKING, like trees do, give your soul more of these times. Shift from there is so many outside factors that influence my life to go inward and focus on my perceptions of these outside factors. Maintain focus on your own steadiness. When you feel trust in your soul, you feel like they are on your side, you are being supported, you are being protected. Tap into the feeling of standing in nature as often as possible, especially when you are not in nature. FEELINGS of faith can happen simply by closing your eyes and seeing white...pivot your thoughts as often as possible when you are feeling hopeless, IT IS NOT ABOUT GIVING UP, it is about finding better feeling thoughts around trust, safety, and confidence. RELAX!

As she found peace, allowing her vision to expand, she saw green leaves, and the symbolism of the green leaves represents growth. The green leaves of spring and summer depict hope, renewal and revival as we celebrate our own changing of the seasons. To further enhance her journey, she saw herself shaking hands with a tree. She felt told to allow herself to not only see what is happening above the ground, but underground as well, see the roots coming together in a handshake as a symbol for internal cooperation and making a deal towards self-acceptance.

After our session, she saw a dietician, and the first thing she told her was to RELAX!!!!!! Literally, the message she received from her inner being.

RELAX INTO YOUR DESIRES.

Primary Imagery: Evergreen Trees

For my client who wanted to FEEL THE FEELS:

When finding oneself, you may also be finding your own self crying. With this client, I invited her to see tears as the release of resistance, offering a powerful return to your desired frequency.

She had planned a trip with her boyfriend, and they ended up going their separate ways prior to this grand hotel adventure. Although her heartbreak wanted her to stay home, she was still dead set on proving to the world and herself that she could go with or without him. She was compelled to follow her inspired nudges. One important component to interject here is that when our inner being is not in agreement with a path for us, knowing our inner being loves us unconditionally and is infinitely intelligent, the decision to go will not feel good. As Baschar so beautifully states, one's path should feel lit up. With this decision to go, she strongly felt her inner being was aligned with her going, yet her desire to stay home was stronger.

She also didn't want to cancel her hotel because she didn't want to pay the cancellation costs. This is a reminder to believe in the power of an ENERGETIC EXCHANGE and always expect the money to come back.

As she debriefed with me, I could feel all of the split energy she brought with her on the trip.

She checked into the hotel and at dinner that night she realized she had misplaced her wallet. THAT WAS IT, she was going home. THIS IS EPIC.

The Universe delivered to her exactly what she desired...WE ARE DELIBERATE CREATORS, be intentional not through effort but through flow.

On the way home, she desired a donut from this place that was known for its yumminess. She went in and realized they were cash only, and realized she didn't have a means of paying either way because she had no wallet. Two men there witnessed her coming to this awareness and bought her a donut!! OF COURSE THEY DID!! She had entered the "ASK IT IS GIVEN" phase, her desires had naturally come to fruition, her trip was canceled and here a donut was purchased for her.

She went home and cried. PURGED.

While with me, she initially called it the worst weekend ever. What if it is the best weekend ever? She was in awareness of her creator's efforts, she purged. She felt the feelings, but most importantly, she realized her power as a creator. EVERYTHING she desired happened.

INTENTIONAL CREATION.

BUT IT GETS BETTER... She began to appreciate it with the following affirmation: "Isn't it awesome to know I will receive my wallet from a blessed stranger," she was detached from any outcome, and she backed her manifestation with pure intentions. Within days, there she was with a phone call from a kind person who said they would love to safely send her the wallet they had found.

Thoughts become things. She left this call believing that her inner being desired her to reaffirm she is indeed a POWERFUL CREATOR.

THE UNIVERSE IS A GOOD LISTENER.

For my client who was trying to find herself:

A situation between my client and a family member came to a head where strong emotions were involved. This client felt guilty and all she could see was her family member crying as she looked back on what happened. For her, witnessing her sister cry activated deep emotions around guilt. Within the despair of desiring to find herself separate from the grief, she immediately saw fireworks. Fireworks can represent the release of repressed feelings... where dreams are related to happiness and celebrations. As we allowed for the divine unfolding of the layers around this, we arrived at some very empowering awarenesses:

1. One never has to envelop other people's emotions.
2. When witnessing another person's tears, it can be natural, knowing that the tears represent a change for the individual, and we should never interfere with another individual's personal journey. In this particular case, the tears were the fireworks, they were the celebration...the person was allowing emotions in as opposed to being detached which was normally the case. The other family member was actually emotionally present, and the tears were evidence of this.
3. As you see others changing around you, you also can give yourself permission to change if the moment allows for personal expansion.
4. Instead of feeling guilty that another person is crying, one can feel compassion yet know that your own steadiness is everything. Stay connected by staying steady.
5. You can see a partnership between the two of you-you are co-creating a journey together and you can see one another as cooperative components in each other's lives. Yet there is divine power in being completely autonomous as you co-create with the Universe.

6. There is a connection with our loved ones, and that is why you care, foster the connection with them as long as you can still foster your connection to your inner being.

7. When faced with other people's grief, it is acceptable to stay energized and transformed.

YOU ARE NOT OTHER PEOPLE'S EMOTIONS.

Primary Imagery: Fireworks

For my client who just quit her job and desired FAITH OVER FEAR:

She just quit her job, and even with all of the uncertainty... immediately her symbolism became the sun.

What an empowering starting point for those changing their life's path, like the sun, she asked herself, what SELF am I outwardly showing to others?

Upon quitting her job, her ex immediately said, "Isn't this a stupid time to quit your job?" Others demonstrated grave concern with questions like, "Should I be worried about you?"

With the desire to quit your job or change courses, there is most likely an inner path that feels more lit up by feelings of happiness and peace. By changing gears and leaving a situation causing you stress, you are giving yourself the gift of freedom. BREATHE. Breathe in deep breaths. When she allowed for mental stillness, we arrived at a beautiful download and inner guidance around other people's judgments, we moved from fear to faith with: I CAN BRING IT ALL BACK TO THE NOW. This statement is pure empowerment... as she stepped into her power, she realized it's not about the past, it is not about the future, it is in the present moment, in this moment, she can allow for her steadiness. Her knowingness was soothed with further awareness that any fears she was experiencing was her old self trying to protect her. She found feelings of security with the perspective: RIGHT HERE, RIGHT NOW, is all that matters, this moment is all I need. Give me one example, when fear solved something for you, she heard. She was reminded that when we trust our intuition, and listen to our inner being, and we follow our inspired impulses, we are on the right path. We can't get it wrong. The Universe not only knows our path, the Universe already has us on the right path. The only thing we have to do is find better feelings and thoughts that are a vibrational match to our desires.

Here is her juiciest nugget of all and it speaks to all of us, when others question our actions, we can OBSERVE, NOT ABSORB. We can observe our critics through the reframing lens that shifts from fear to faith, "I have so much faith in my personal decisions, and I know my critics are simply practicing a perspective that is not aligned with my own." With all of this, isn't it nice to know that the weight of your happiness does not rest on the shoulders of others? Isn't it nice to know you can find happiness from within instead of seeking external validation? Isn't it nice to know that when we come from a place of unconditional love for ourselves and our inner being, we can allow FAITH to triumph over FEAR?

Her Divine Download: This life is your ARRIVAL PARTY, not your SURVIVAL PARTY, show up as the person you want to be, and if that means quitting your job, you have an entire Universe that has your back.

THE UNIVERSE IS YOUR WINGPERSON.

Primary Imagery: The Sun

For my client who was facing his truths...

His opening statement was, "I have anxiety..." and his inner being immediately offered beautiful photo memories, one where he had just won a championship game, he saw himself standing at a podium, and feelings of confidence flowed through him and he said these words, "From a place of confidence, comfort, and contentment; I can be in the moment and not care and allow things to bounce right off of me. As a result, I feel lighter."

As we continued to deconstruct the feeling of anxiety, another photograph appeared, this one was of a nine-year-old version of him wrapped up in a crocheted blanket, and this gave him feelings of total security. Why was this so powerful? His recent wobble around anxiety was around an upcoming zoom group call, where he had some escalating feelings of "What will people think of me?" The impact of this thought was a direct result of some bullying he was on the receiving end of while growing up. HERE IS THE WOW FACTOR...the imagery of the crochet blanket where one end is on a chair and the other is on the bed gave him the feeling of being in a fort, his fort was his "comfort zone". Suddenly, there was a realization that he can create his *comfort zone* within his new reality. Then there was this, "I can give myself permission to allow images and memories of my past that show a version of me that is happy, confident, and secure."

When we "face our truths", especially at the individual level, to what part of your life's story are you placing your focus upon? There is no doubt in my mind, his inner being beautifully delivered an image of him standing at the podium because we can allow memories in where we didn't feel anxiety.

He desired more moments where he was confident, where he felt total confidence, and where he felt no anxiety. He was creating a new comfort zone.

His ultimate download: When I enter a new situation where I feel the initial spike of anxiety, I know I can bounce right off any situation. When I am less reactionary, I can do more things I LOVE. I can allow for more feelings of calm instead of that initial spike of anxiety. To be completely carefree feels so good. I CAN STAY AS IS. Circumstances do not have to alter my state. I have the power to walk away, I have the power to be empowered, and instead of things happening to me, I can allow new circumstances to happen for me.

THIS IS NOT A THEM ISSUE, THIS IS A ME ISSUE.

Primary Imagery: Purple clouds

This Ending is your Beginning

I do not fix problems. I fix my thinking. Then problems fix themselves.

— Louise Hay

My highest desire is to be remembered by the new stories I tell about my life, not how I used to tell them. I set the intentions for everyone around me to hear my new story. I encourage you to do the same. For all of us, our thoughts matter, our emotions matter, our feelings matter, and our language matters. The peace and joy we find within and through the words we share is and will continue to be reflected in our physical reality. By living inside out and outside in with an awareness of our emotions, we honor ourselves as powerful creators.

I am living proof and there is ample research to suggest that the sensible use of imagery can be most beneficial when we take the time to connect by going inward. I believe that by aligning to our inner being through daily meditation, we are in the receiving mode for infinite insight and wisdom.

In closing, I offer full appreciation towards the Universe for allowing itself to write through me for our collective healing and our leveling up. By tapping into the powers of our imaginations, I simply cannot imagine a life better lived. Hear me see you. You are worthy of having a journey of personal possibilities on life's playground.

Let us all remember who we are and who we are meant to be. Whereas we may have forgotten the power of visual imagery in our lives as a child, let us all remember its power as adults.

There is room for so much celebration here as well. When we devote time to raising our own personal consciousness, we raise the level of collective consciousness. By allowing for a better you, you are changing the world. While some may not still believe that happiness is a choice, I know that happiness can spread.

The bottom line, deal with your inner shit, you can do all of the manifesting techniques but if you don't shift your energy, release resistance, cut the cords of what is weighing you down, you will continue to limit your power as a creator. Calibrate and celebrate, you being here right now, in this very moment, is not a coincidence, it is a cooperative incident orchestrated by the Universe as you move closer to all of your desires. It is no longer SHIT HAPPENS, it is SHIFTS HAPPEN.

Feel an unconditional group hug from your higher self and your inner child while remembering the Universe always provides. Say YES to you, more like HELL YES, to the life you desire by having the courage to go inward first. Thank you for playing with me in the new paradigm, where your outer journey becomes an inward one. It feels good to feel good... joy is your natural state of being.

Stay plugged into your inner energy.
Allow alignment to be a priority.
Release resistance through meditation.
Listen to your inner voice and make it your own.
Your future self and your higher self believe in you.
Follow your inspired impulses.
Live in peace, not disturbance.
Be in the receptive mode.
Here I am. Here you are.
Live in appreciation.

You have a calling.
Live in awareness.
Be still and know.
Be an observer.
Surrender.
Be open.
Listen.
Trust.

You are more than you are.

About the Author

Liz Landon, M.Ed. CH, is a Certified Hypnotist and Law of Attraction Coach who has received several recognitions for her devotion to soulful practices. As one who has spoken at professional conferences and been a featured guest on podcasts, her accolades include profound and life-changing testimonials because of the impact others experienced with her divine messages and spiritual guidance.

Once Liz learned that all negative emotions are personal invitations to visualize and internalize paradigm shifts that effortlessly allow for feelings of relief and freedom, her life changed. Her sacred space is warmly reserved for guiding people into their personal power through the spiritual eyes of the imagination.

As Liz facilitates people towards the energy of possibilities knowing manifestation is an energetic dance with the Universe, her clients *release resistance* as they step into the vibrational vicinity of their highest desires. Although she shares intimate stories from her own life's path, she knows your personal journey is yours. By simply following your flow and reframing practiced perspectives towards your highest good, you create a new life's story.

For speaking engagements, live seminars, virtual summits, exclusive access to Liz's group coaching program, as well as booking an intuitive embodiment consultation using Liz's RELEASE RESISTANCE FORMULA, please contact her at releaseresistancewithliz@gmail.com.

www.ingramcontent.com/pod-product-compliance
Lightning Source LLC
Chambersburg PA
CBHW070506160726
48003CB00004B/1452